BABY LOVE

BABY LOVE
A Tradition of Calm Parenting

MAUD BRYT

A Dell Trade Paperback

A DELL TRADE PAPERBACK
Published by
Dell Publishing
a division of
Bantam Doubleday Dell Publishing Group, Inc.
1540 Broadway
New York, New York 10036

If you purchased this book without a cover you should be aware that this book is stolen property. It was reported as "unsold and destroyed" to the publisher and neither the author nor the publisher has received any payment for this "stripped book."

Copyright © 1998 by Maud Bryt

All rights reserved. No part of this book may be reproduced or transmitted in any form or by any means, electronic or mechanical, including photocopying, recording, or by any information storage and retrieval system, without the written permission of the Publisher, except where permitted by law.

The trademark Dell® is registered in the U.S. Patent and Trademark Office.

DESIGN BY JOEL AVIROM
DESIGN ASSISTANTS: JASON SNYDER AND MEGHAN DAY HEALEY

Library of Congress Cataloging in Publication Data
Bryt, Maud
    Baby love: a tradition of calm parenting / Maud Bryt.
        p. cm.
    ISBN 0-440-50822-3
    1. Parenting–United States. 2. Infants–Care–United States.
I. Title.
HQ755.8.B79 1998
649'.122–dc21   97–51409
                                                          CIP

Printed in the United States of America

Published simultaneously in Canada

September 1998

10 9 8 7 6 5 4 3
RRD

QUANTITY SALES

Most Dell books are available at special quantity discounts when purchased in bulk by corporations, organizations, or groups. Special imprints, messages, and excerpts can be produced to meet your needs. For more information, write to: Dell Publishing, 1540 Broadway, New York, NY 10036. Attention: Director, Special Markets.

INDIVIDUAL SALES

Are there any Dell books you want but cannot find in your local stores? If so, you can order them directly from us. You can get any Dell book currently in print. For a complete up-to-date listing of our books and information on how to order, write to: Dell Readers Service, Box DR, 1540 Broadway, New York, NY 10036.

To my mother,
Johanna van Riel Cinader

ACKNOWLEDGMENTS

Thank you to my mother, Johanna van Riel Cinader, who taught me, slowly, as I was ready for it, how to take care of my daughters when they were babies. Her patience, her wisdom, and her sense of humor about it all are what I strive for and what I hope to share with others through this book.

Thank you to Susanne and Greg Daniels and Jill Altshuler, who came up with the idea for this book one sunny morning over coffee and then told me to do it. Thank you also, Susanne, for collaborating with me on the outline even though you had a full load at the office and a newborn at home. This book has the good fortune to have been started when Helena Louise Daniels was born and finished when Zachary Miles Altshuler was born.

Thank you to my sister, Emily Woods, who as usual understood completely and had faith in what I wanted to do; and to Emily and Cary Woods for getting excited about this book and leading me to Mort Janklow and Cynthia Cannell, and then Tifanny Richards, who were kind enough to take me on.

Thank you to Cynthia Cannell, whose calm and insight kept me on track and led me to my editor, Mary Ellen O'Neill.

Thank you to Mary Ellen O'Neill, who cares about the little things also, and knows when to laugh and when to say no. Her children are lucky. Thanks also to Mike Shohl, who ran out into the rain.

To the early readers of the manuscript: Susanne Daniels, Jill Altshuler, Bartley Bryt, Michelle Lee, and Johanna Cinader.

To Sarah Jeffers, Louise Harpman, and Eve Jordan Combemale, who found babies for me to photograph.

To Eve Jordan Combemale, who contributed her sense of style to the photographs when I needed it most.

To Joel Avirom, Meghan Day Healey, and Jason Snyder, who turned a stack of photos and a stack of well-edited text into a beautiful book.

To the McLaughlins, the Newmans, the Gallaghers, the Daniels, the Altshulers, the Jeffers, the Colin Kleins, the Combemales, the Grunebaums, the Levys, the Guthries, the Koons, the Barclays, the Grossmans, the DeLaurentises, the Andersson-Dubins, the Meaders, and the Mosses who shared their beautiful babies with me.

To my friends Kathleen O'Hagan, Sarah Jeffers, Francesca Lynch, and Ridgely Biddle for going through the baby and toddler years with me as stay-at-home moms and seeing through the piles of diapers all over our houses, spit-up on our shoulders, and endless pots of pasta to where the humor and love are.

Thank you to my daughters, Catherine and Natalie, who didn't get to have much say in whether or not I did this project, but whose good health and good cheer made it possible. They continue to teach me how to take care of them.

And, most of all, thank you to my husband, Bartley, for his unwavering encouragement, his love, and his willingness to step in when I stepped out.

CONTENTS

Introduction *xi*

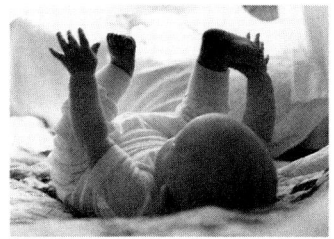

NURSERY
1

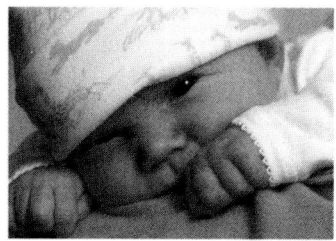

CLOTHING
9

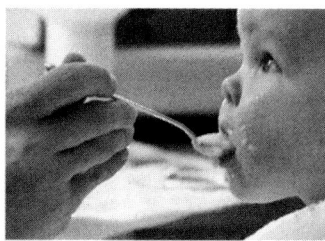

FOOD
17

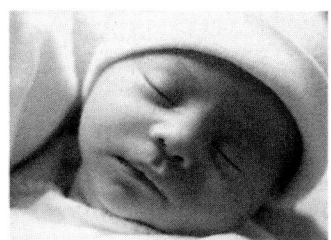

SLEEP
37

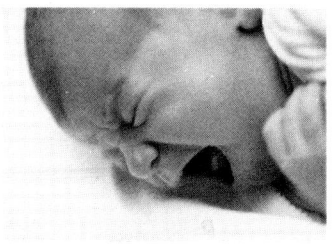

CRYING
51

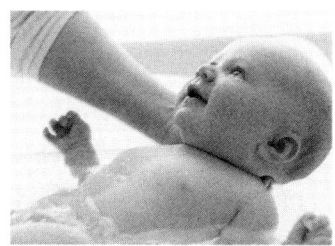

BATH
59

DIAPER
71

PLAY
77

OUTINGS
91

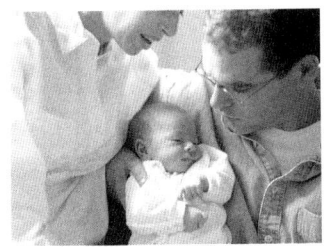

FAMILY
103

ILLNESS
115

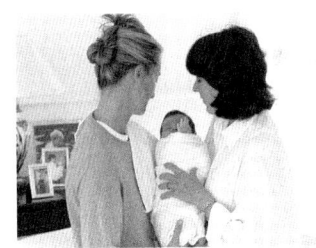

VISITORS
121

INTRODUCTION

Welcome to parenthood!

Throughout time, couples have been having babies, and until very recently they were surrounded by family and community members and trained helpers. These people would help them for the first few weeks and teach them what they needed to know. There would be an affirmation of parenthood and the importance of what was being done. The new mother's work would be shared. There would be inside jokes about how the world really works and also a shared feeling of awe at the gift of a new life.

Now it seems we're all checking development charts and growth charts and sleep charts and calling our babies "good" if they don't cry and pacing around our homes by ourselves with our little newborns, wondering if anybody else has noticed that life is made up of poop and spit-up and leaking milk.

With this book I hope to convey a sense of community, to teach you how to do a few things that will make taking care of your baby easier and more effective. I want to share a few tricks of the tradition, which I guarantee your baby will love. I want to help you see how joyous and difficult and sometimes funny being parents can be.

With the photographs I hope to inspire you to see taking care of your baby as a beautiful, natural thing to do, and also to show what some mysterious things such as front-carriers, bassinets, lying-down positions, and receiving blankets are.

Most of all, I want to help you get into the habit of trying to see things from your baby's perspective. So many difficult situations in parenting can be avoided or remedied by making an effort to understand what our children are thinking or feeling, what they need, and it all starts when they're babies. It helps to keep a goal in mind—to meet our babies' needs while guiding them gently toward fulfilling their potential—but it also helps not to worry too much when things change or don't go the way we plan. How a baby grows and matures is a mystery, which to a large extent can only be wondered about.

My husband, Bartley, who is a pediatrician, and I come from long lines of loving parents who take parenting very seriously. What I know about taking care of babies I learned from my mother, whom our children call "Oma," the traditional word for *Granny* in Holland. Throughout this book you will hear Oma's voice, which is really her mother's voice and *her* mother's voice and is becoming my voice. My mother and her mother and her grandmother were all nurses and midwives in Holland back when midwives taught new parents how to care for their babies over the course of two to six weeks, but the valuable techniques and attitudes I got from them and their husbands were not developed in hospitals. They learned, and passed on, how to make parenting a joy in damp, small homes in Holland, where they knew that to thrive as parents you have to keep your perspective and keep things comfortable for you and your baby.

I hope you read this book snuggled up in your bed or on a couch with a blanket. Let's get started!

NURSERY

Oma likes to tell a story about when she and my father were in Switzerland skiing when their first baby was a few weeks old. Her mother had come along to care for their baby while they were skiing. When the hotel didn't have a crib ready, my grandmother just pulled out a drawer from the bureau, wiped it down with a damp washcloth, folded up a clean blanket to line the drawer, and then took the baby from my mother's arms and laid him down to rest. "Good," she said. This story is a good antidote to the catalogs full of baby gear for "the nursery." All you really need is a clean, safe place for your baby to sleep. The rest is not strictly necessary, so pick and choose what you want, but don't lose any sleep over it.

    Another thing you want to keep in mind is that your baby will be a child soon, so the less babyish and the more childlike you make the more permanent fixtures of the room, the better. The crib will give way to a twin bed, and the bureau will just be a bureau, not a changing table, within a couple of years.

    So buy what you need and want to make the room function well and feel cozy, but leave space for the things that your baby's personality will inspire when she's older.

EQUIPMENT

The following elements make a good nursery:

- ☐ Bassinet, basket, or corner of a crib (make sure crib meets current safety standards)
- ☐ Bureau with a separate, concave, waterproof changing pad on top
- ☐ Row of hanging pegs near changing table
- ☐ Rocking chair or comfortable armchair
- ☐ Twin bed
- ☐ Curtains or "blackout" shades for windows
- ☐ Lamp with low-wattage bulb

It's nice for your baby to have a small place to sleep at first, which is why a lot of people use a bassinet or basket for the first few weeks of a baby's life, but a corner of a crib can be just as cozy. If you set up the bumper in a smaller rectangle around one corner of the crib and place the crib in the corner of the room, it can feel very snug for your baby.

Make sure the surface of the bureau you choose is large enough to fit the changing pad and also some supplies next to it. You'll need a stack of diapers, a spray bottle, a box of tissues, some ointments, and space for a clean change of clothes. Also make sure that the bureau with the pad on top of it is a comfortable height. The top of the pad should be an inch or two below your elbow in order for diaper changes to be comfortable for you.

It's helpful to have a row of pegs within reach of the bureau on which to hang clothes that have been barely worn, pajamas, damp washcloths or towels, or anything else that you don't want to put in a drawer or the laundry. These hooks will continue to be useful throughout your baby's childhood.

A rocking or glider chair is useful for feeding a baby while sitting up, for reading stories, and for soothing a crying baby, but an armchair can do just as well.

If space permits I recommend a twin bed in a nursery, for a few reasons. First of all, it's handy to have a place for you to lie down. It's a good place for nursing or bottle feeding, for playing with your baby, or cuddling. In the middle of the night you or your spouse can sleep peacefully in your bed while the other feeds the baby in the nursery and then falls asleep there. This is also a way for your baby to associate those comforts with her own room, not just yours. In addition, it's handy to have a bed set up as a couch and bed for baby-sitters. Finally, your baby will need a twin bed eventually, so why not start getting some use out of it now?

Shades and curtains are useful for helping your baby to go to sleep or to keep sleeping when it's light outside during the summer, and they're also helpful for blocking drafts in the winter.

A low-wattage bulb in a lamp helps keep nighttime diaper changes and feedings dim and soothing.

LINENS

These are the basics you should start with:

- ☐ Waterproof mattress casing
- ☐ Two flannel-lined rubber pads, crib-sized
- ☐ Three fitted crib sheets
- ☐ Two cotton blankets
- ☐ One cotton quilt
- ☐ One washable wool or polyester fleece blanket
- ☐ One cotton bumper
- ☐ Ten "burp pads" (cloth diapers)
- ☐ Two extrafirm pillows for your back and under your arm while feeding

Oma insists on pure cotton and wool for babies to ensure a good flow of air around the baby. She also prefers a knit, or stretchy, bottom sheet for the crib so that if the baby sweats the sheet remains soft, not cold and slick.

The cloth diapers will come in handy as a clean layer between baby's head and your or someone else's shoulder, on a couch or quilt placed on the floor, in the stroller, and in front of your baby's face in a front carrier. Cloth diapers are also useful under your baby's head in the crib for fewer sheet changes.

Before your baby is born it's a good idea to gather any old blankets and towels that you have and wash and dry them well. Fold them and put them in a pile under some tissue paper in your closet. Once you have your baby these will come in handy for making changing tables out of surfaces around your house, throwing down for play mats, and as cushions for washcloth baths.

EXTRAS

Extras you might want:

- ☐ Mobiles
- ☐ Mural; wall hangings

It's good to strike a balance in a baby's room between stimulation and rest. A well-placed mobile turning in a breeze can be soothing and interesting for a baby. Every inch of a wall covered with wall hangings and shelves of toys might be overwhelming and will collect dust. You don't need to have a "motif" for the nursery. Rather, you can pick and choose a couple of nice elements that you like and think are playful and soothing for your baby, then add to the room slowly as you come to know your baby's, and then child's, interests.

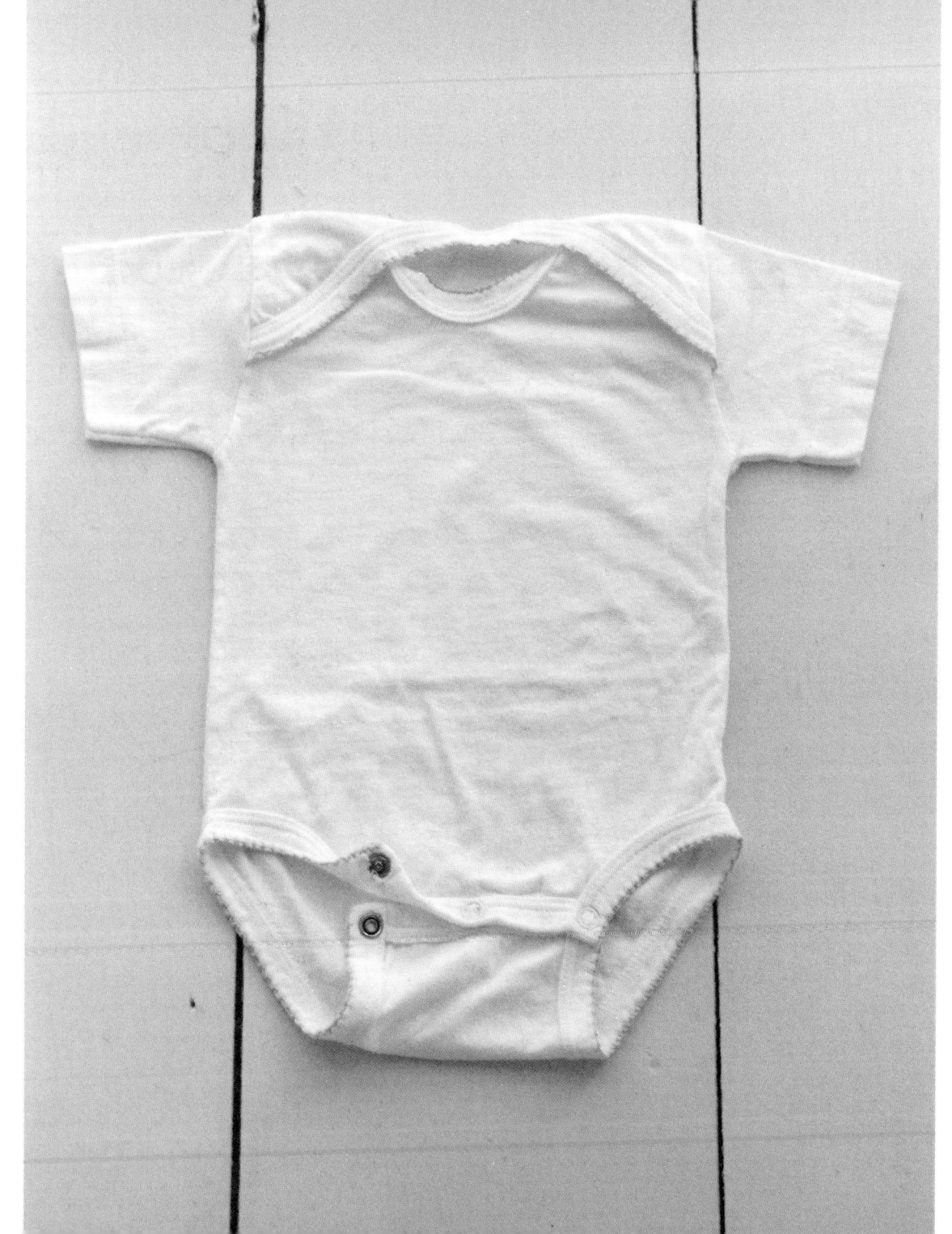

CLOTHING

What is it about those little socks that on their own can make you want to have a baby? Is it that they're so small or that it's so ridiculous that such a small person could really need socks? With those little arms and legs, tiny little neck, and beautiful round head, any clothes seem unfit for a new baby. But babies do get cold, and they do need clothes. The best you can do is keep the clothes comfortable and easy to put on and take off so that your baby will be kept warm but not bothered by his clothes.

When coming up with a list of clothing, have in mind comfort for sleeping and eating, since that is how your baby will spend most of his days and nights. This means keeping waistbands and extra buttons or snaps to a minimum.

Oma likes a clean, breathable cotton layer against your baby's skin, under any other layers you think he might need. Always make sure you clean your baby's clothes well, rinsing and drying them thoroughly before using them against his skin.

YEAR-ROUND CLOTHES

The following is a lineup of year-round standards, which you can add to as your baby grows:

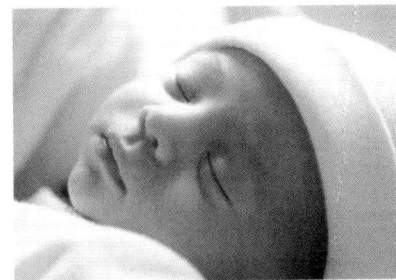

- ☐ Nine undershirts, 6-month size
- ☐ Three stretchy knit caps
- ☐ Three pairs baby socks and/or booties or baby "shoes"
- ☐ Four "no-waistband" outfits
- ☐ Two two-piece outfits, mix-and-matchable
- ☐ Three receiving blankets

The most basic elements of your baby's wardrobe will be a diaper and a cotton undershirt, short- or long-sleeved depending on the season. Wraparound undershirts are good for newborns because you don't have to pull them over their still-soft heads. They come with ties or snaps that close in the front. For the first three months of life count on three undershirts a day, times however many days you go between laundry days, especially if your baby has very liquid stools or spits up a lot. Get the six-month-old size from the beginning because they're fine for a newborn and he'll grow into them in no time. One popular kind of undershirt snaps over the diaper like a bodysuit. These stay smooth against your baby's skin. Oma reminds you to watch out for hot snaps when you take your baby's clothes out of the dryer.

You should always have a thin, soft, not-too-tight stretchy cotton cap for your baby, no matter what season it is. After a bath, in the morning, under a fleece or wool cap outside, when he's getting sleepy and his fingers feel cool, are all good times to put on a cap. Get three, and one will always be clean and ready.

Unless it's very warm your baby will need something to keep his feet warm. Oma has a theory about feet, and it goes like this: If your feet are warm your tummy will feel good, and if your feet are cold you're bound to have a tummy ache. If you don't believe it, pay attention to your own feet and tummy for a while. In any case, don't forget about your baby's feet and keeping those tiny little toes warm. Soft socks are perfect. Shoes for little babies are really just glorified socks and should be flexible and soft.

Of course no one knows for sure, but I am convinced that a baby's tummy feels better without a waistband around it. One-piece coveralls ("stretchies") that cover feet also are probably the most comfortable next layer after the undershirt for your baby. They don't put pressure on your baby's tummy and don't get twisted with wriggling. Outfits that close with snaps on the shoulder and diaper-opening snaps are the best. Buttons or snaps up the front or back might press into your baby's skin when he's sleeping or sitting in an infant seat, so make sure any snaps are cloth-covered and smooth.

Two-piece outfits can be convenient when your baby repeatedly soils the lower half or upper half of his outfit. You can change the half that is dirty without completely undressing your baby. Also, if it's warm he can wear just a shirt or just shorts or pants. Make sure the waistbands are fabric-covered and aren't too tight.

Receiving blankets are squares of smooth or stretchy cotton that have many uses. Most importantly, you need them to swaddle or make a *pakje* (see later chapter on "Sleep") out of your son, but they're also useful as a play mat for him, as a clean shoulder pad for visitors and yourself, as a lightweight blanket for a nap, or as a makeshift sun shade in the car. For expert *pakjes* for newborns, Oma insists on nonstretchy receiving blankets. With them you can make the kind of tight *pakje* that newborns love. Stretchy receiving blankets are good for making looser wrappings for babies six weeks and older. Don't buy too many if you're going to receive gifts, because many people give these as gifts.

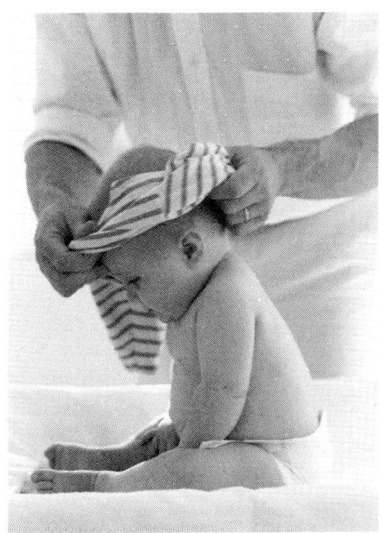 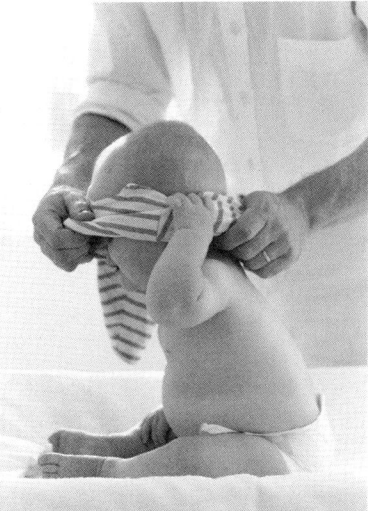 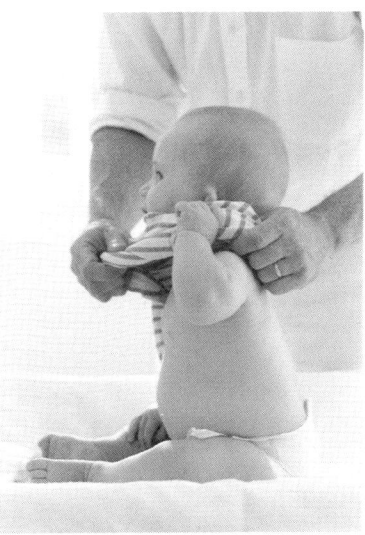

HOW TO PUT CLOTHES ON A BABY

Before you start to dress your baby, make sure you have everything you need within reach. Then lay him on his back and start with his head and work your way down.

Whether he is on a bed or a changing table, always make sure you keep one hand firmly on his tummy whenever you reach for something.

When trying to pull clothing over his head it makes things easier if you stretch the neck opening and hold it apart with your hands in a ring so that his head will be restricted for only a short time. Pull the clothes down over his head starting at the crown.

To put on sleeves and legs of pants, bunch up the sleeve or pant leg into a ring, reach in, and gently pull your baby's hand or foot through by the wrist or ankle.

Oma wants you to make sure your baby's undershirt is smooth and that his sleeves are pulled all the way down if he's wearing another layer on top. Socks should be pulled up or rolled over neatly, and collars should lie flat. Babies spend a lot of time lying down, and it's uncomfortable to be lying on bunches or wrinkles of fabric.

SEASONAL CLOTHES

For the summer you'll need the following:

- ☐ Two broad-brimmed sun hats
- ☐ Two lightweight but long-sleeved and long-legged outfits for outings

In general it's good to dress your baby loosely and in light-colored clothes in the summer so that air can circulate near his skin and so that sunlight and heat will be reflected off him. Get your baby used to cover-ups now so that he'll wear them as a matter of course when he's older. A hat will do a lot to protect his head, face, and shoulders from the sun and is essential for babies with sensitive skin. Get two so that one can fall into the water or onto a dusty road.

Don't forget about your baby's hands and feet when covering up from the sun. You can pull lightweight, long sleeves over his hands while he's riding in the front carrier or stroller and then roll them up when he's ready to play.

For the winter you'll need the following:

- ☐ One jacketlike bag or bunting ("baby bag")
- ☐ Two nonitchy polyester fleece hats with ear flaps and a visor

Babies lose a larger percentage of heat through their heads than adults do, especially if they don't have much hair, so it's very important to keep your baby's head covered in cold weather. Equally important are fingers and toes. Mittens are difficult to keep on. Baby bags that completely cover hands and feet are ideal, but if you use a regular snowsuit, either use a large enough size so that you can pull the sleeves and legs over your baby's hands and feet or make sure the sleeves always overlap the mittens and the pant legs always overlap the boots. A front carrier inside your own jacket, with your baby's feet tucked inside, is a snug, warm place.

For the fall and spring it's a good idea to bring along the following whenever you go out:

- ☐ Lightweight jacket or baby bag
- ☐ Wide-brimmed hat

Even if the weather seems stable, it's a good idea to have a jacket on hand for a sudden change of temperature or if you end up being out longer than you expected.

Also remember to watch out for sunburn in cool weather when the temperature might mislead you to think that the sun's rays aren't strong.

FOOD

When thinking about food for your baby it's helpful to keep in mind the end result: to have her eat good, full meals at the same time as the rest of your family, with help from one or two snacks if necessary. In order to reach that stage you need to discover what your newborn baby needs in terms of frequency and amount of food and then, as her stomach grows over the course of time, gently guide her toward larger and less frequent meals. Clocks and numbers of ounces can be useful tools for keeping track of your and your baby's progress, but try not to let them be the guiding force.

     Oma would say: If your baby's good and hungry when she's fed, she'll eat all she should.

CHOOSING TO BREAST-FEED YOUR BABY

Breast feeding is the healthiest, most convenient, most economical, and ultimately the easiest way to feed your baby. It helps her immune system, it may prevent breast cancer in you, it forces you to relax periodically, and the milk is always with you and at the right temperature no matter where you are, which is no small thing. But it does take commitment and energy. You need to learn the correct way for your baby to latch onto your breast, you need to make sure you get enough rest, and you need to drink a lot of fluids. At the beginning it can seem difficult, but very soon it feels good and the frequency of feedings gets more and more manageable.

The only equipment you need for breast feeding is:

- ☐ Four nursing bras

Choosing to breast-feed your baby doesn't mean you have to give up your mobility either. Once your milk supply is established (after six weeks or so) you can store milk in the freezer for bottle feeding and reap the rewards of both bottle feeding and breast feeding. You'll be able to grab your daughter and an extra diaper and go anywhere at the drop of a hat without cleaning out bottles and measuring powder into a container. If you pump your breasts at work for your baby to drink the following day, as many mothers do, you'll have the satisfaction of knowing that even though you're apart for the day she is drinking your milk.

HOW OFTEN TO BREAST-FEED YOUR BABY

Most breast-fed babies need to be fed every hour and a half to two hours at the beginning. Their stomachs are small and the milk is easily digested. Breast feeding provides your baby with a very frequent source of comfort and soothing food. The more your baby sucks from your breasts, the more your breasts will be stimulated to make more milk (see "How Your Milk Supply Increases," later in this chapter), so that when her

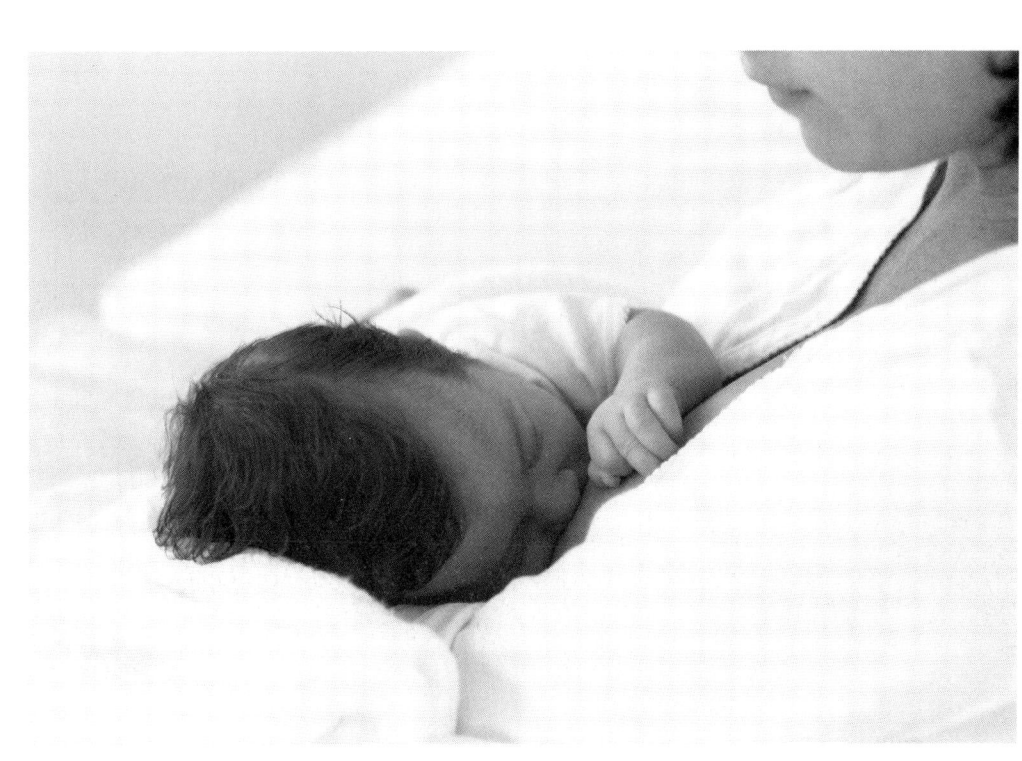

stomach grows bigger you will be able to provide more milk. For the first month of your baby's life your baby and your breasts shouldn't go more than four hours between the beginning of feedings, even if she's asleep. Gently wake her up for her feedings if necessary by changing her diaper or rubbing her back.

Gradually, your baby will have more and more awake time when she doesn't need to be feeding. Either she'll wake up, feed, and then be awake for a little while, or she'll wake up, be happy for a little while, and then need to feed and go to sleep again. It is during those times that you can play with her, give her a bath, or go for an outing.

You can ease your baby into a predictable schedule by responding with food more quickly when she has waited longer for a meal and more slowly or only after trying other responses if it has been less than an hour and a half since the beginning of the last feeding. On the other hand, if you're tired or not drinking enough fluids, or if your baby is having a growth spurt, she just may need to feed very often.

By a month to three months of age she may be able to—and should be allowed to—sleep for six to eight hours in a row at night with no feedings. It helps to maximize your hours of sleep by feeding her right before you want to go to sleep.

REST WHILE YOU FEED

You may have heard of football holds, cross-body holds, and sling holds with relation to breast feeding. You've probably seen pictures in catalogs of women sitting in rocking chairs with a pillow under their arm and a stool under their feet. When I had my first baby a well-meaning woman told me I had to nurse sitting up and holding my baby with her head in my hand. Well, the last thing I wanted to do after giving birth was sit, and she kept rolling off the side of my arm. I quickly went back to what Oma had taught me in the hospital and what has worked for generations.

Oma says: Drink a glass of water, then lie down! The idea behind all the different "positions" for breast feeding is that you need to make sure you drain all of the different areas of your breast, but if you pay attention you can do that while lying down.

There is *no* reason why a new mother should have to sit up to nurse. You need to rest to recover from birth and to make milk. You don't want to fall into a cycle of tiredness/not making enough milk/having to nurse constantly. Since you'll be nursing about ten times a day—three of which you'll be in bed for anyway—you may as well learn right now how to nurse effectively lying down. There will be plenty of months for nursing while cooking dinner with the other hand later, but for now you need to rest.

Oma suggests that you scan the newspaper every morning and mark three or four articles that you want to read at some point during the day. Then put the newspaper, folded up to the article, near the chair or bed where you'll be feeding your baby so that you have something quiet to do while you're feeding her. This has the added benefit of keeping you up to date on things so that you don't feel like a diaper-and-milk machine.

HOW TO BREAST-FEED LYING DOWN

Oma's two-pillow setup is comfortable, allows you to hold a book or telephone with your other hand, and assures good support of your breast for complete emptying.

- ☐ Wash your hands.
- ☐ Place one pillow on top of the other like a staircase parallel to your body.
- ☐ Lay a clean burp pad or cloth diaper on the lower pillow.
- ☐ Lie on your side with your breast on the clean cloth on the lower pillow and your head on the upper pillow.
- ☐ Make sure your whole breast is supported well by the pillow. Imagine the milk needing to flow from the base of your breast all the way to the nipple, and make sure that's a straight line.

While you're doing this keep your baby away from your breast—down near your stomach, laying next to you on the bed—or if possible being held by someone else until you're ready.

When you're all set up:

- Lay your baby down next to you on her side with her head level to your breast, and touch the corner of her mouth with your nipple. This will cause your baby to open her mouth wide.

- When her mouth is wide open, pull your baby *quickly* toward your breast and make sure your whole areola (all of the pink skin)—or as much as will fit—goes into her mouth. Her gums should press down on the outer edge of this area to push the milk toward the nipple.

This is called "latching on," with good reason. If you allow your baby to suck or chew on your nipple, it will become sore. Once you feel a stinging fullness in your breast (called the "letdown") and her jaw is moving rhythmically, you know that she is sucking well and swallowing milk.

Get to know how much she can suck at a feeding, so that you can make sure to stop halfway through and switch breasts. To get your baby off your breast:

- Stick a clean finger into the corner of her mouth to break the suction.

- Then remove your breast.

After you're finished with the first breast:

- Give her a chance to burp by holding her against your shoulder and gently patting her back.

Oma also recommends changing your baby's diaper and then washing your hands before switching breasts. Most babies have a bowel movement when they start eating, so if they're going to, they usually have by the end of the first breast. Also, if you've already changed her diaper, and she falls asleep by the end of the second breast, you won't have to worry about waking her up to change her diaper or about her sleeping in a dirty diaper. If your baby gets sleepy by the end of the first breast, having her diaper changed and being carried over to a sink or being put down in her crib to wait so that you can wash your hands (which is important) will wake her up for the second part of her feeding.

When you're ready:

- ☐ Switch the burp pad to the other side of the pillow steps and align your other breast.

It's *very* important to keep track of which breast you offer first at a feeding. Your baby will suck more vigorously at the beginning of each feeding, and in order for your breasts to be equally stimulated to produce milk, you need to alternate the starting breast. The traditional way to keep track is to have a pin on your bra strap that you move midway through the feeding, but I just used a ring that I switched back and forth between my hands. A bracelet, a Velcro tab on your bra, anything that you can switch left to right will work, but don't rely on memory. An additional reminder of which breast you need to start with can be on which side you wrap your baby into a *pakje* (see the chapter titled "Sleep").

HOW TO BREAST-FEED SITTING UP

If you need or want to breast-feed sitting up, it is easier in a chair with arms or with a firm pillow to help support your arm that is holding up the baby. Another thing to try is sitting cross-legged with your knee holding up your arm. As with the lying-down position, it is important that you make sure that there is a straight line from the base of your breast through your nipple to the back of your baby's head.

HOW TO ENCOURAGE THE LETDOWN OF MILK

Sometimes it's difficult to relax enough for your milk to come down. If this happens, take a deep breath, close your eyes for a moment, and then look at your baby. Try to forget about what you were doing or what you need to do, try to forget about what time it is or when the last time you fed her was. Make sure you're in a comfortable position, relax your jaw, your shoulders, and your legs. Take another deep breath.

HOW YOUR MILK SUPPLY INCREASES

The basic concept behind how your breasts work is they will make as much milk as your baby sucks for, with a few days' lag time. For the first few days not much will come out while you're adjusting to the new demand, and then all of a sudden you'll have plenty of milk. This will happen every time your baby has a growth spurt and needs more milk. She will suck longer and more frequently for a few days, and then your breasts will adjust their supply. Don't get discouraged during these periods and think your schedule is falling apart. Rather, be proud that your baby is growing thanks to your milk and wants more. Drink a lot of water all day long, wait a few days, and you'll be back on a schedule.

Oma is very strict about not tinkering with this delicate mechanism by giving your baby formula out of fear that she's not getting enough calories. If you drink plenty of fluids your breasts will meet the demand, but if your baby is sated by formula, she won't continue to suck as hard, and you won't make more milk. Consult your pediatrician if you are convinced that your breasts can't make enough milk, but always give it a few days first. "No tinkering" goes for using frozen breast milk also.

HOW TO BREAST-FEED IN PUBLIC

Breast feeding in public is an art form. You need to learn how to do it if you don't want to feel chained to your house. The basic concept is to create privacy. There are clothes available made expressly for nursing in public, but you can always use a cloth over your shoulder. Any receiving blanket is the right size to make a little tent. Just drape it over your shoulder and all the way over your baby.

The art to this technique is having the right facial expression while you're nursing. Of course, if you're at your friend's house it doesn't matter, but if you're at a park or on an airplane (and nursing is great for takeoff and landing), you don't want to draw attention to yourself as a vulnerable mother–baby bundle. The key is not looking too often at your baby. If you're reading or looking at something else, other people will too and you'll feel less self-conscious.

COMBINING BREAST AND BOTTLE

Once your milk supply is established, by about six to eight weeks (although this is variable and you should check with your pediatrician), it's a good idea to get your baby used to taking one bottle a day so that you can leave her with a family member or baby-sitter occasionally, so that you can take a break from breast feeding occasionally, and so that your husband can feed her when he wants to. For storing breast milk, express your milk right after a feeding or half an hour later, but don't try expressing within an hour of your next feeding time. You are most likely to be short on milk in the late afternoon when you're most apt to be tired, and that's the best time to use your stored milk or formula (if you do it consistently) in a bottle. Giving the second-to-last feeding of the day with a bottle will also give your breasts a chance to store up plenty of milk for the last feeding of the day, helping you and your baby get a good night's sleep.

BOTTLE FEEDING EQUIPMENT

If you're bottle feeding exclusively, you'll need the following:

- ☐ Four four-oz. bottles
- ☐ Eight eight-oz. bottles
- ☐ A nipple, a nipple ring, and a cap for each bottle
- ☐ Bottle brush and nipple brush for cleaning
- ☐ Formula
- ☐ Lead-free water

Powdered formula is the least expensive, and it is good for traveling and outings because you can bring a bottle of sterile water and the powder separately and then combine them right before feeding. There are containers with four compartments in which you can carry a day's worth of powdered formula with you.

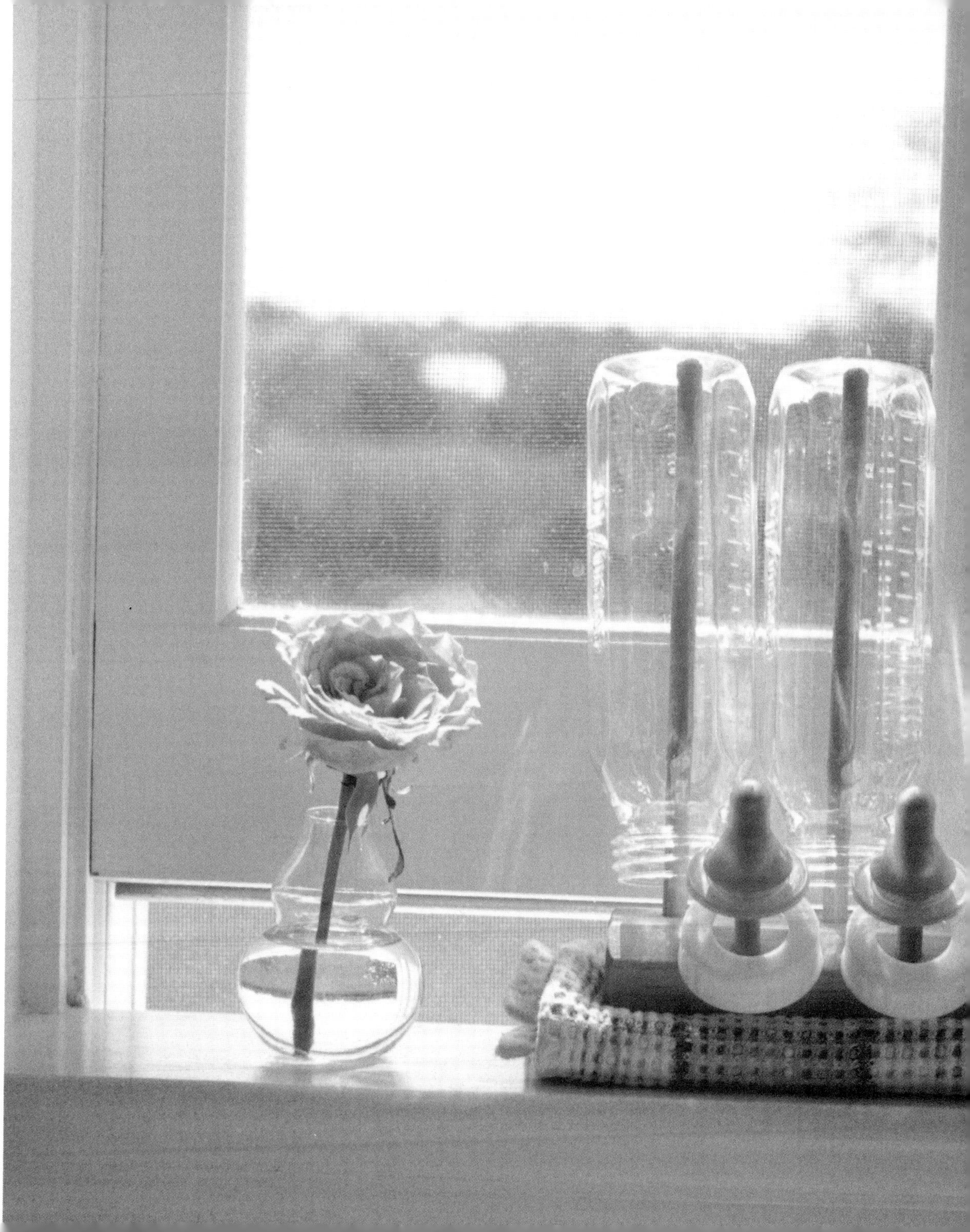

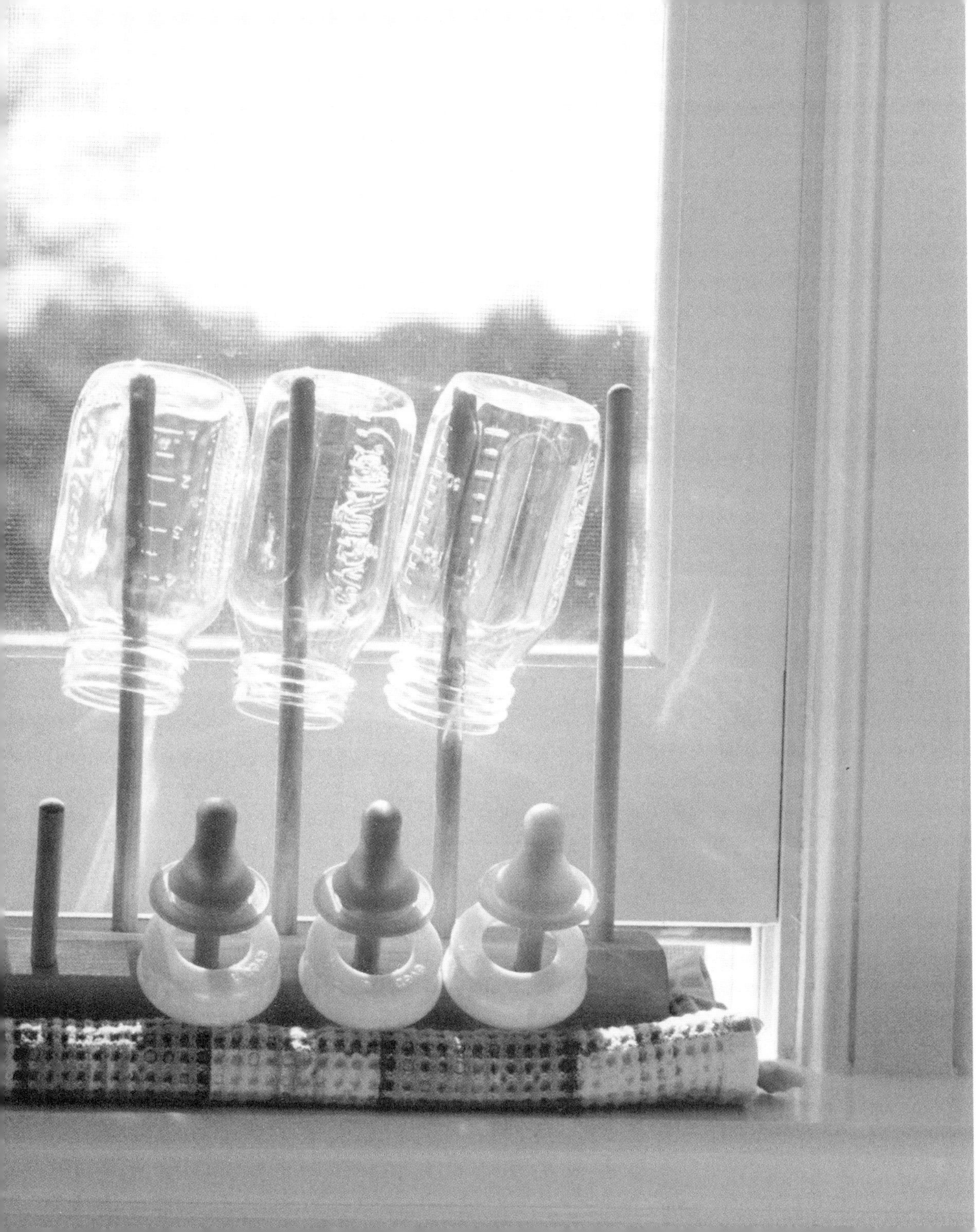

HOW TO GET FORMULA READY

Start by washing the bottles, nipples, and nipple rings well with soap and water, making sure to clean inside the nipples with a nipple brush. Next, boil the equipment in water for five minutes and then let it dry on a clean rack. Mix a day's worth of formula at a time with preboiled and then cooled-off lead-free water, and store it in the refrigerator in a clean container with a top.

Once your baby is two months old and you don't need to boil the bottles or the water anymore, you can put the bottles in the dishwasher, the nipples in a basket with a top, and use any clean, cold lead-free tap water to mix the formula. Just be sure to check the nipples every time you wash them for wear and tear and for formula stuck in the nipple hole. Make sure they're not sticky (this means the latex is breaking down), and make sure they are not stretched out of shape (this means they could break soon and be a choking hazard). Buy new nipples frequently.

HEATING A BOTTLE

You will probably read everywhere not to use a microwave to heat your baby's formula or breast milk, but it really is the easiest way to do it. You just have to be careful, because you can burn your baby's mouth and throat if you don't do it correctly. Follow these guidelines:

- ☐ Find out how long to heat the bottle by experimenting, but never assume that the bottle will be heated exactly the same every time.
- ☐ Make sure you mix the formula or breast milk very well after heating by shaking it upside down and by swirling it.
- ☐ *Always* test it on the inside of your wrist after mixing and pay attention to the temperature.

HOW TO BOTTLE-FEED

Once you're sure that the formula or breast milk is uniformly a good temperature, sit or lie down with your baby in a quiet place, if possible, and offer her the bottle. If she doesn't open her mouth, try touching her cheek with the nipple and she'll probably turn her head toward it and open her mouth.

Make sure the nipple is full of formula or breast milk when feeding your baby so that she doesn't suck in too much air. There are disposable, collapsible liners you can buy that ensure that as little air as possible gets into your baby's stomach. If you're not sure if she is getting any milk out of a traditional bottle, listen carefully and you will hear a fizz sound as the liquid goes into her mouth and is replaced with air in the bottle. If you don't hear the fizz and you don't see any little bubbles going into the bottle from right around the nipple ring, then loosen the nipple ring until she is able to suck the liquid out of the bottle and you hear the fizz and see the bubbles.

If you don't use all of the breast milk or formula in a bottle that has been sucked from, you must throw it out after an hour, because by that time bacteria will have begun to grow in the bottle.

INTRODUCING SOLIDS

At around four to six months of age your baby will be able to start eating solids. Check with your pediatrician about which foods to begin with and in what order. Usually they suggest rice cereal because it's the most gentle and easily digested grain. Make a small dab of cereal very liquid with breast milk or formula, and then offer it to her on a small, rubber-tipped spoon. If she pushes it out of her mouth instead of swallowing it after a few tries, try again the next day. If she still can't swallow it, then wait a week or two and try again. Soon enough she'll be demanding to hold the spoon herself and flinging food across the room, so take your time and enjoy the slow process.

Once your baby has mastered rice cereal and your pediatrician says it's okay, you can try smoothly ground cooked carrots or squash to give her a taste of sweet vegetables. You can introduce a new food every week or so, but do it one at a time so that you can detect a food allergy if one appears. Once you have a few vegetables and fruits in your repertoire, take a morning to cook and blend food and then freeze it in ice cube trays to last the rest of her first year.

By six or seven months of age, your baby will be ready to gum little pieces of banana, dry cereal with holes in it, and crackers. She will be able to sit in a chair with a tray and feed herself, to both of your delights.

Up until a year of age, think of her as "practicing" on solids and don't put pressure on yourself to have her eat any specific quantity of food. It is a time for your baby to explore textures and tastes and to practice swallowing. She may eat a lot of solids and cut back on milk, or she may just experiment with solids and rely on milk for her nutrition. As long as she is happy and growing, you can be assured that she is getting what she needs.

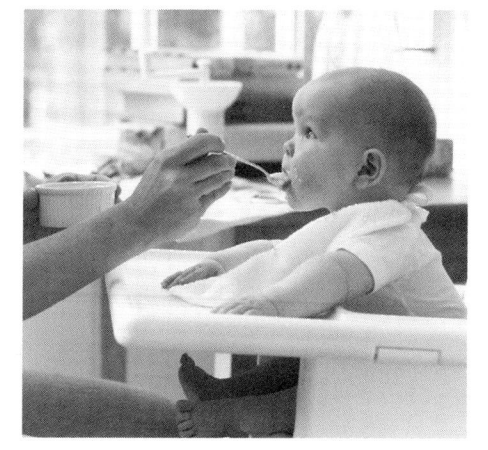

HOW TO COMBINE SOLIDS AND MILK

When you feed your baby solids, do it as part of a meal of formula or breast milk that you're feeding her anyway. Otherwise, you'll be feeding her too often during the day and she'll never get really full or really hungry. Oma suggests introducing solids at the evening meal. That is when your milk supply will be at its lowest if you're nursing, and nursing or not, you want your baby to get the most calories before nighttime to help her "last" longer without food while she's sleeping. At any given meal start with the solids and then let her drink as much breast milk or formula as she needs. Gradually add a meal a day at which she eats solids. Eventually, of course, she will eat proportionally more and more solid food and drink proportionally less and less breast milk or formula. By about a year or a year and a half, she will be eating a meal with a cup of milk as a beverage.

THE CUP

Switching from the breast or a bottle to a cup should be done gradually, as your baby becomes ready for it. Once she can sit up in a high chair (around six or seven months), you ought to give her a chance to learn how to use a cup. There may be a time when she absolutely will not drink formula from a cup but will be willing to try water from a cup, and then there will be a long time when you can offer her the cup first and then finish up with the bottle. And then you'll find that she's eating enough between solids and the formula she's getting from the cup that you don't need to offer her the bottle at all for three out of five meals. Or your baby may accept the cup and say good-bye to the bottle overnight. The goal you want to keep in mind is for her to eat her meals from whatever vehicle she is ready for.

GIVING YOUR BABY WATER

There are many times when you might want to offer your baby some water—when ill with a fever, in hot weather, or between meals. Oma recommends offering water to a baby early on to get her used to the taste. Boil the water for five minutes to sterilize it and then let it come to room temperature. Offer it in a bottle. Once your baby is two months old you can give her clean, lead-free bottled or tap water.

35
FOOD

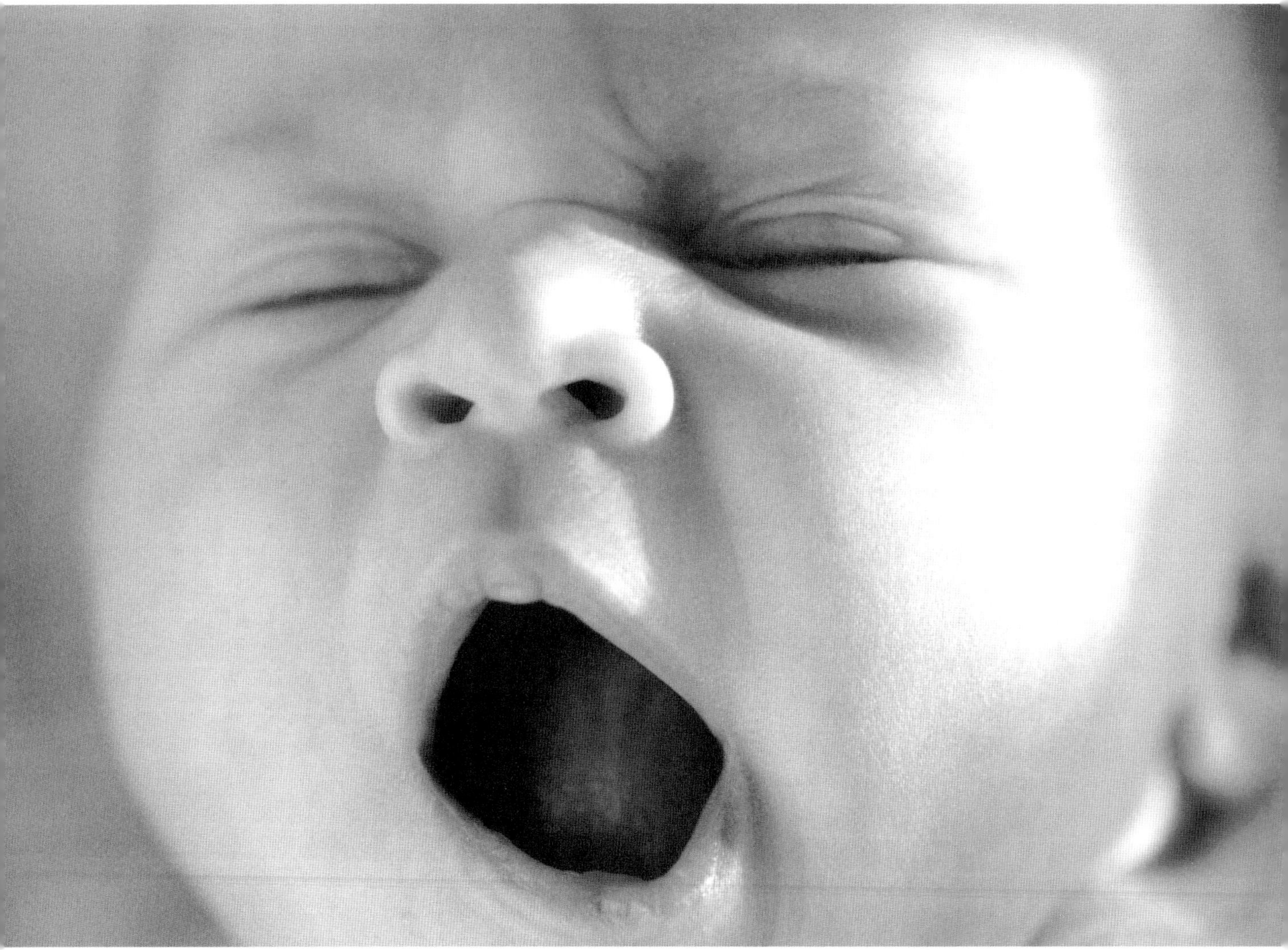

SLEEP

Before you have your first baby, sleep is something you fit in. You sleep after you're finished with everything else, you sleep as a luxury on a weekend morning, you catch up on sleep later. When you have a newborn, sleep is gold. You have to become sleep smart. You have to know when to sleep and how to do it even if your house is a mess and you haven't returned phone calls for a week. You're exhausted from the physical exertion of birth, frustrated by having to learn how to do so many new things, and elated at having a baby. You think sleep can wait, but learning how to relax and sleep when you need to—and how to help your baby relax and sleep when he needs to—will affect more than anything else the tone of your experience as a parent. "Go to sleep!" Oma would tell me firmly, and now I tell it to you.

ADAPTING TO YOUR BABY

You have to try not to pay too much attention to numbers and the clock these first few months. You and your baby are a team, and you need to adapt to him before he'll be able to adapt to you. You need to sleep with him during the day so that you can recover from the birth, make milk, and attend to him when you need to at night.

The average amount of sleep a newborn takes is sixteen hours. This is only an average, which means that your child may need anywhere from ten to twenty-two hours of sleep. In other words he'll sleep when he needs to, and you'll just have to wait and see what his pattern will be. One constant is that newborns' stomachs are small. They can hold only about two hours of breast milk or three hours of formula at a time when they're born, so to begin with they need to eat around the clock. This means they can sleep only in short spurts. An ideal sample schedule might be two periods of four-hour sleep at night and then two or four two-hour naps during the day. If you do the math, this means you are feeding, changing a diaper, or helping your baby go to sleep during every one of your waking hours *at the beginning*.

Gradually your baby's stomach capacity will grow, as will his ability to be awake and alert for longer stretches during the day and asleep for longer stretches at night. By three months he will probably be able to sleep for six or eight hours in a row at night and he'll take a few predictable naps during the day, so you will be able to sleep on a grown-up schedule soon. In the meantime, give in to it and make the most of it, all the while learning what your baby needs.

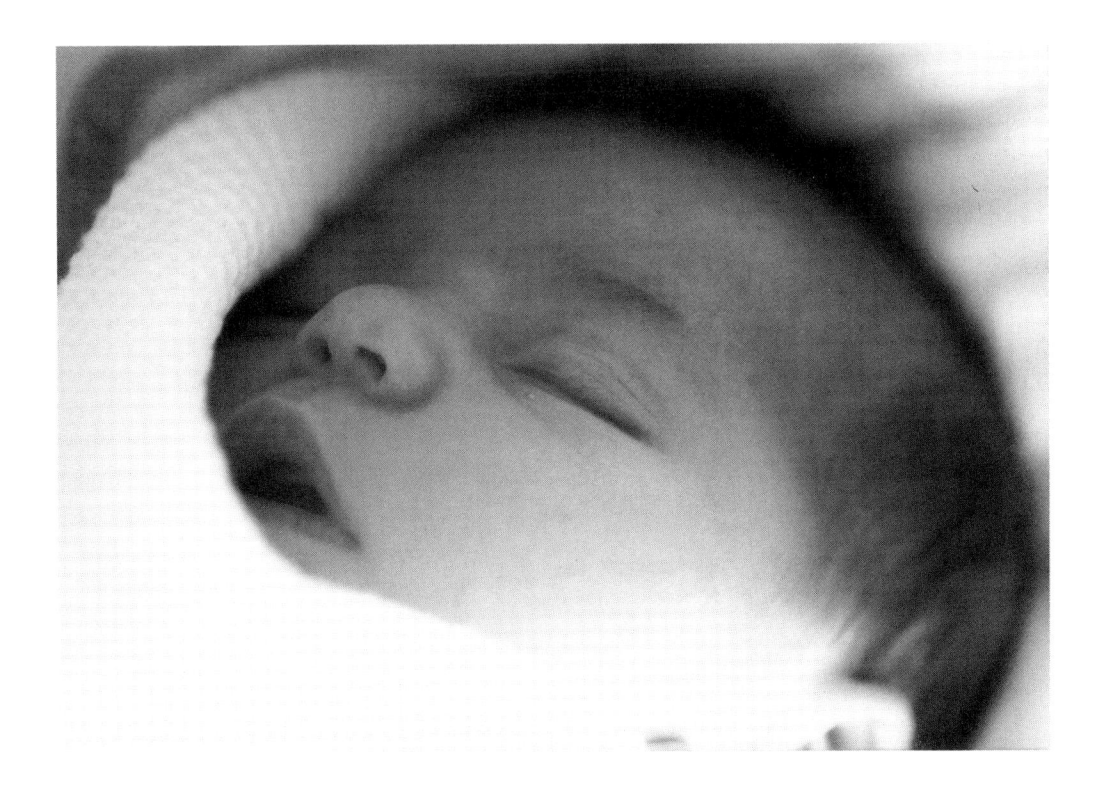

HOW TO THINK ABOUT NAPS

The goal with naps for you and your baby is to have them be a supplement to nighttime sleep but not take away from it. Naps should be taken within earshot of daytime activity and in a shaded but not darkened room. From the beginning babies should sense that daytime is different from nighttime. Experienced parents do this naturally because the siblings set the tone of the house. Unless you live in a palace the baby in the house is going to know it's daytime if there are siblings around. A new parent can get desperate, though, and, trying to catch up on last night's sleep, make the house as dark and quiet as night when it's not. Naps should have a different spirit to them so you and your baby can keep them separate in your heads. This is important later when you want your baby to know that when he wakes up after a nap he gets out of his crib, but at night he goes back to sleep until it's morning.

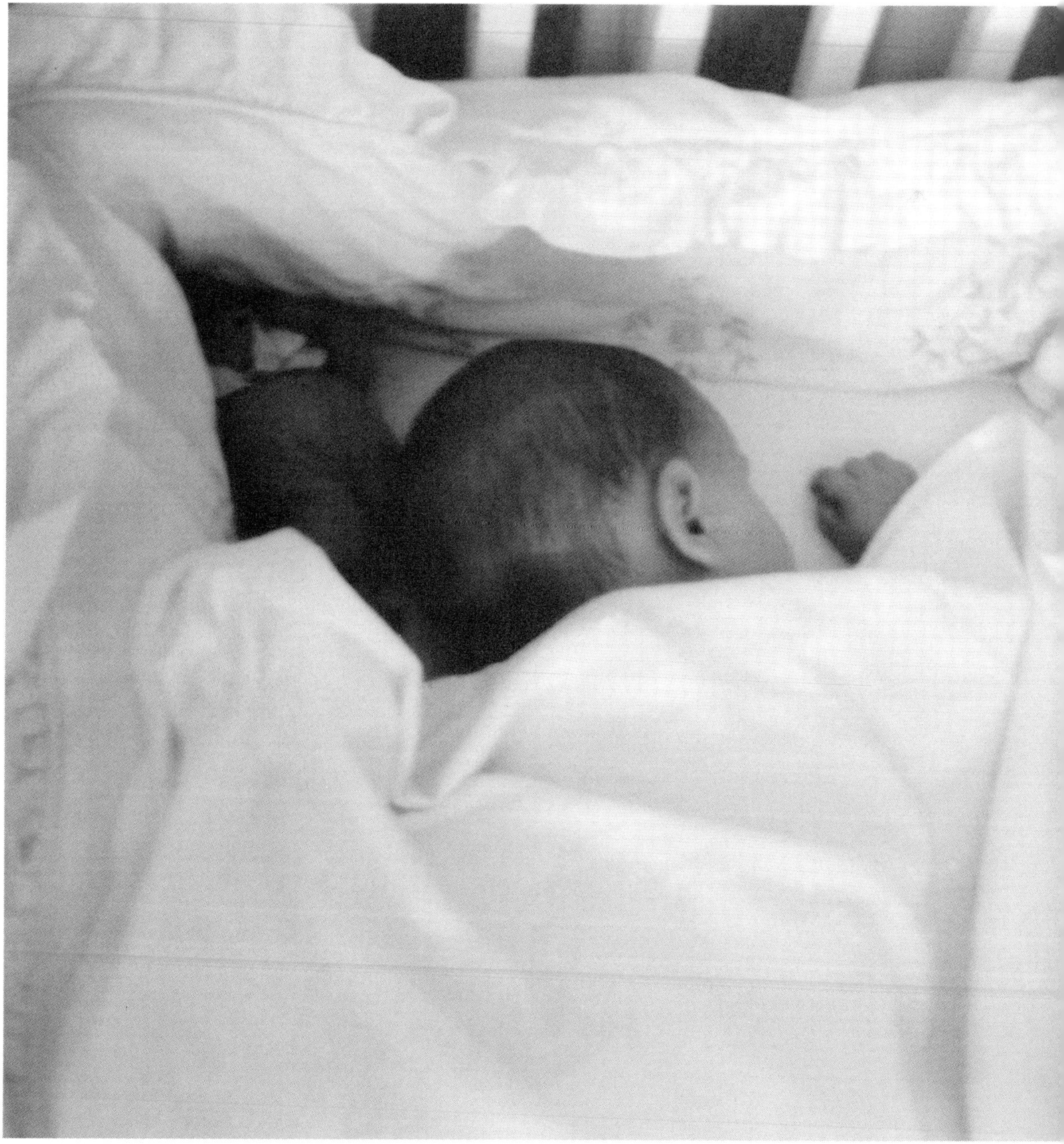

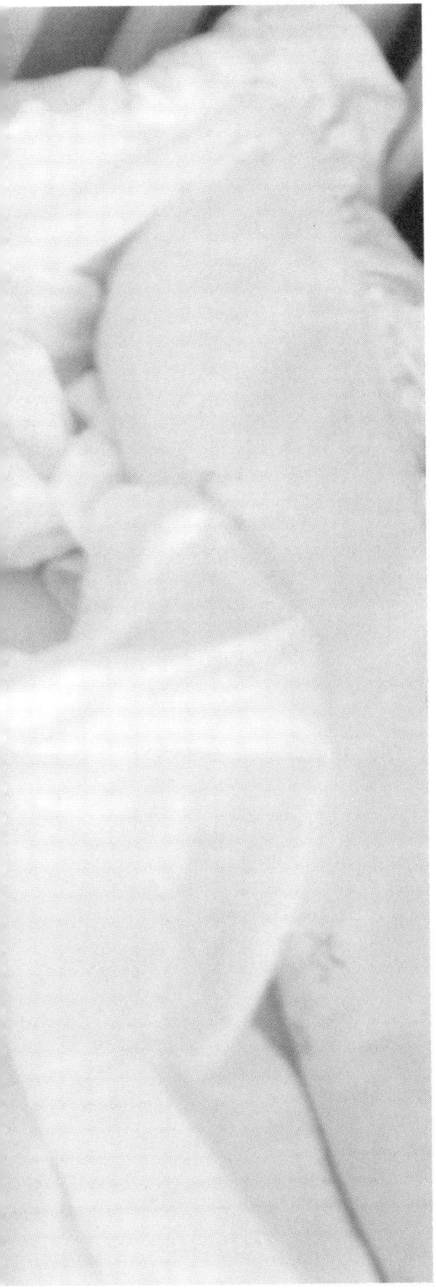
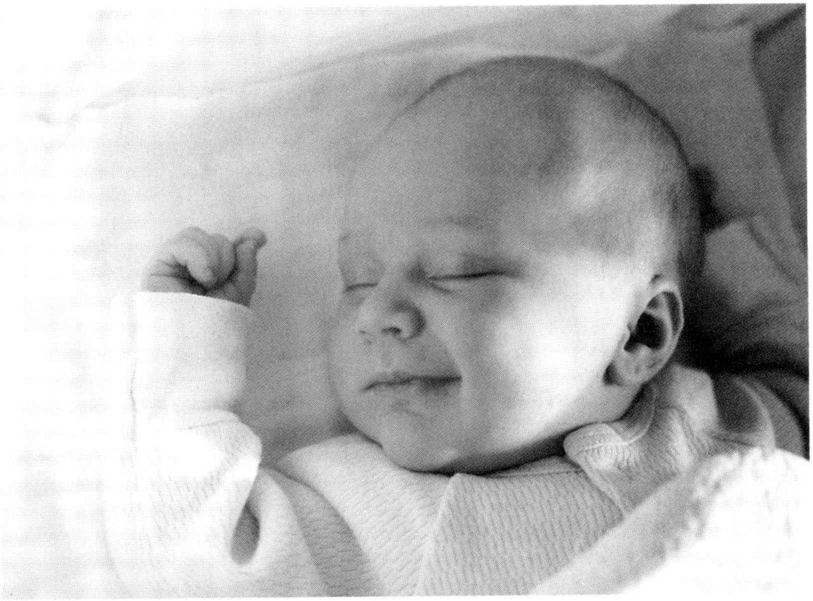

PICK A NAPPING PLACE

You need to pick a napping place for you and your baby. If it's your bedroom, just pull the shades halfway and sleep on top of a made bed instead of in it. Use a lighter blanket on top of the baby and leave the door open. If it's summer, pick a corner of a porch or yard and put a playpen with mosquito netting over it in the shade. On a weekend, ask your husband to take a walk with the baby asleep in a carriage as a nap. All of this will help him sense that naps can be very restful but are shorter than and different from nighttime sleep.

For both of our babies we used our carriage as a roaming crib around the house. Propped up inside or lying down, our babies could keep an eye on us, then when they got sleepy we could wheel them into a quiet corner, put a rolled-up towel behind their back to keep them on their side, and let them fall asleep.

Oma strongly recommends that you have a crib or carriage on all floors of your house. You're more likely to put your baby down when he's tired instead of carrying him around if there's a handy, safe place right there.

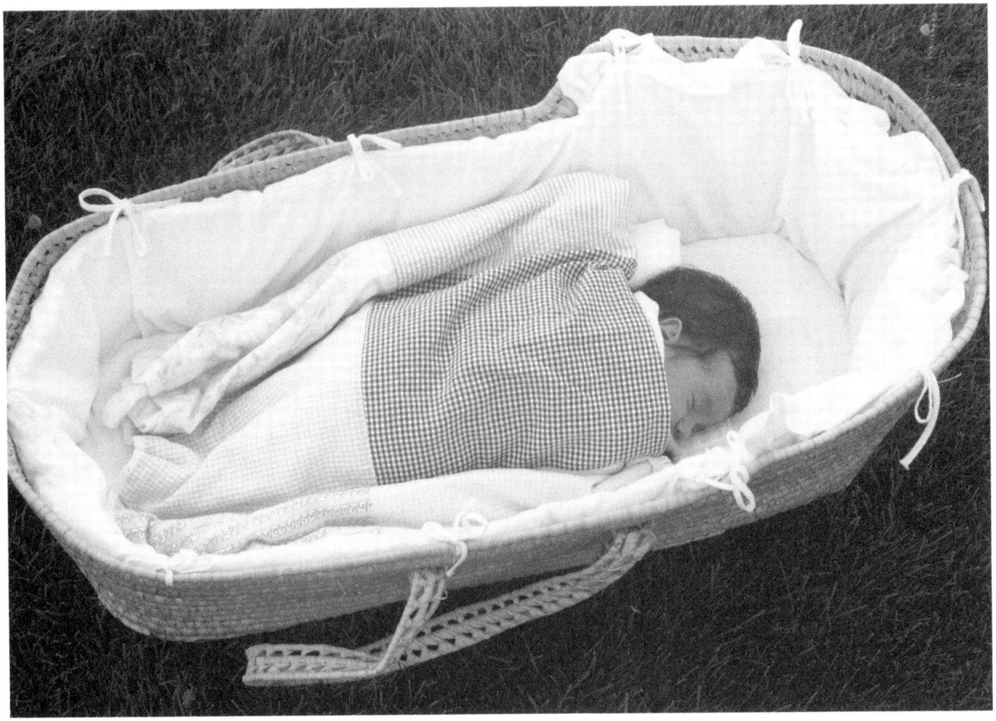

AN EVENING BEDTIME ROUTINE

Once you know your baby is well-rested in general and is well-fed, you can begin to think about a bedtime routine. This may seem ludicrous for a newborn, but it's as much for you as for your baby. You don't want to start habits you'll regret four months from now. You do want your baby to begin to sense that there's a time for everything, and that nighttime is sleep time.

First of all, what is your house like in the evening? Is the TV on loudly? Are all the lights on? Is one of you on the telephone talking or laughing loudly? Are you catching up on vacuuming? Your baby is very alert to what's going on around him. He may fall asleep despite the stimulation, or it may even lull him to sleep, but at some point, when he's six months old perhaps, he'll want to join in the fray in the evening instead of going to sleep. Then you'll have a difficult time retraining him to think the evening is a good time to go to sleep.

Once you decide on a good bedtime for your baby, you need to make sure the one or two hours leading up to that bedtime are quiet. You can't really expect him to be happy and calm with an abrupt change from being stimulated to being expected to go to sleep. He needs a transition time.

Turn off a few lights. Read instead of watching TV, or at least turn it down. Listen to quiet music. You and your spouse should talk over and agree on a bedtime routine together so that you can both stick to it.

Make a bedtime routine that starts early in the evening: bath, pajamas, last feeding, song, sleep. In a few weeks your baby will know in his body, if not in his mind, that he goes to sleep after the song that is after his last milk, which is after his bath. The routine can stay the same as you move his bedtime earlier and he's able to sleep longer at night as he matures.

Make sure, and Oma stresses this, that you don't make a routine that you don't like. It sounds obvious, but it's easy to slip into habits you don't like. Don't carry your baby around for an hour because it made him stop crying once; don't sing a song if you don't like singing; don't give a bath as part of the routine if it's still too difficult for you. Do find a comfortable chair that jiggles in a good way, do read a short board book, do nurse or bottle-feed with your feet up or lying down. Do what you like and do what works, and do it the same way every evening.

A SMOOTH TRANSITION
FROM YOUR ARMS TO THE CRIB

Oma puts a hot-water bottle in the crib before a baby's final feeding so that when the baby is ready to drop off and she puts him down, his bed is as warm as her arms. This worked beautifully for our babies and for the hundreds of babies in Oma's past.

Try from the beginning to put your baby down when he's still a little awake and in the same place he'll wake up in later. Your baby will associate certain sensations with falling asleep. The more you can make his crib the place where he falls asleep, the more likely he will be able to fall *back* asleep there if he wakes up at night.

Sometimes it works if you pat your baby's back rhythmically after putting him down, slowly slowing down to no pat at all. Another trick is gently jiggling the bassinet more and more slowly.

With all of these you want to let him do as much of the getting to sleep as he can by himself. You want to work toward phasing yourself out of the process, because eventually he will need to know how to get himself back to sleep on his own in the middle of the night.

Oma's way of knowing that a baby has really dropped off into sleep is by listening for *snuffeltjes*, or little snores. If a baby has been crying and you finally get him calm and quiet and you think he's asleep, first wait for the *snuffeltjes*. After the second little snore, which usually ends with a sigh, it's usually safe to take your hand off your baby's back.

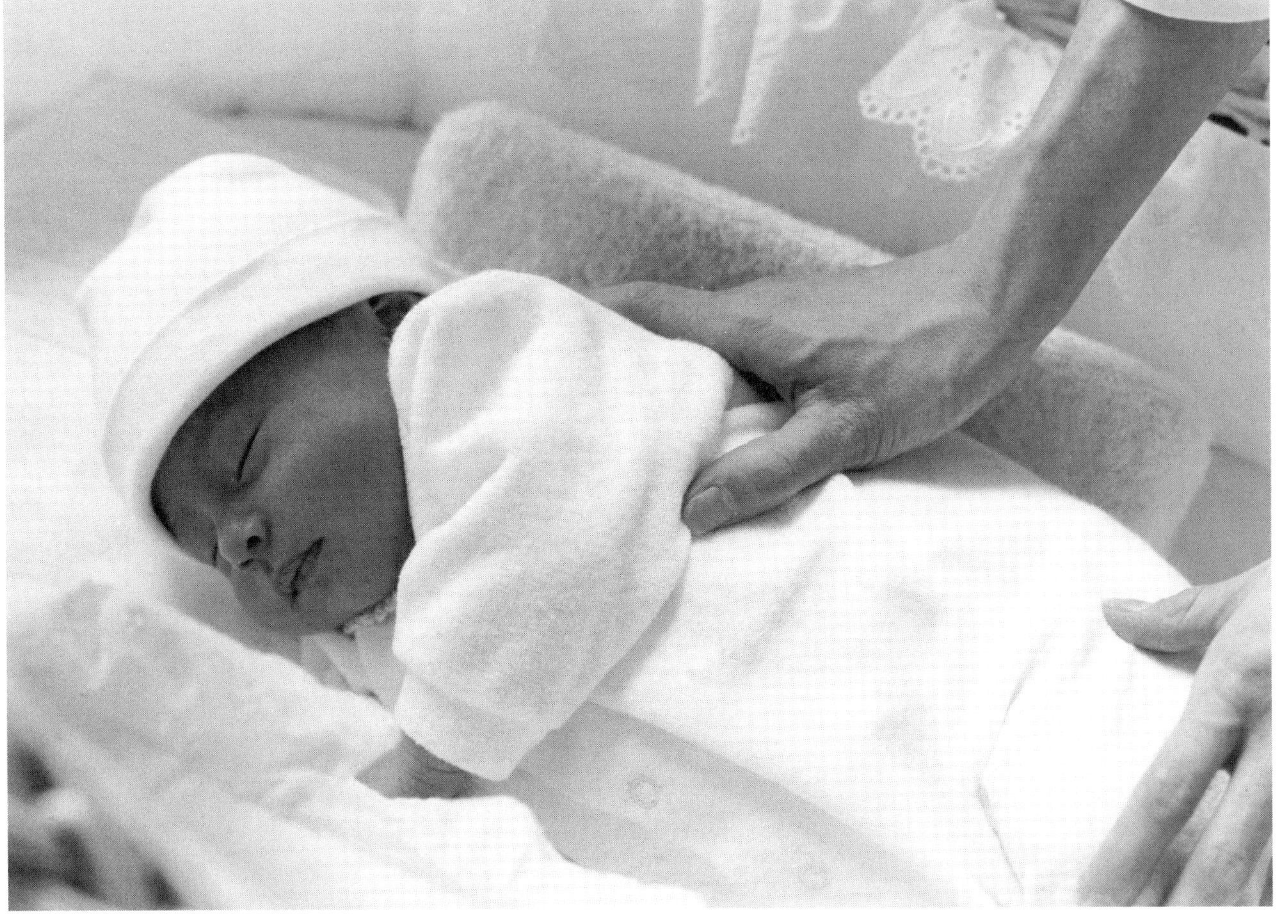

HOW TO HANDLE NIGHTTIME WAKING

The main idea with nighttime waking is to keep your baby as sleepy as possible. Don't turn on lights. Don't start playing with your baby. Try letting him resettle for a few minutes by himself. If he doesn't, go to him and try putting your hand on his back. It's helpful to have a nightlight in his room so that you don't have to turn on a bright light. If he still cries, pull him into your bed or the bed in his room and feed him. Halfway through, burp him and change his diaper so that he'll be awake enough to finish a good, full feeding, but do it quickly. Wash your hands. Then finish the feeding and put him right back in his crib.

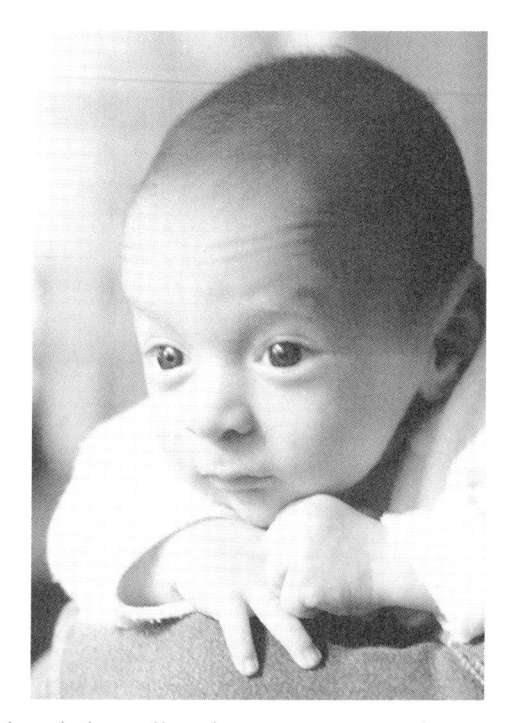

You may have heard of people walking their babies all night, or turning on the vacuum or TV at three in the morning, or turning on all the lights and acting out the itsy-bitsy spider when no one else in the apartment building has turned over for four hours. All of these remedies are short-term and they do usually stop the crying for the time being, but they don't help you get your baby into good habits. Attend to your baby's needs at night, but don't offer him any stimulation.

POSSIBLE CAUSES FOR EXCESSIVE NIGHT WAKING

One way to help your baby sleep better and longer at night is to make sure he gets plenty of activity and stimulation during the day. (See the "Play" and "Bath" chapters.) Do be careful not to overdo this, though, as overstimulation can hinder his sleep. Also make sure your baby gets enough naps during the day. An active and generally well-rested baby has less trouble falling asleep and resettling.

If your baby starts waking up more often at night for a while, it may mean that he's going through a change—a growth spurt, a new tooth. After you've ruled out illness, have faith that he will either return to his normal sleep pattern or establish a new sleep pattern of sleeping for longer stretches very soon.

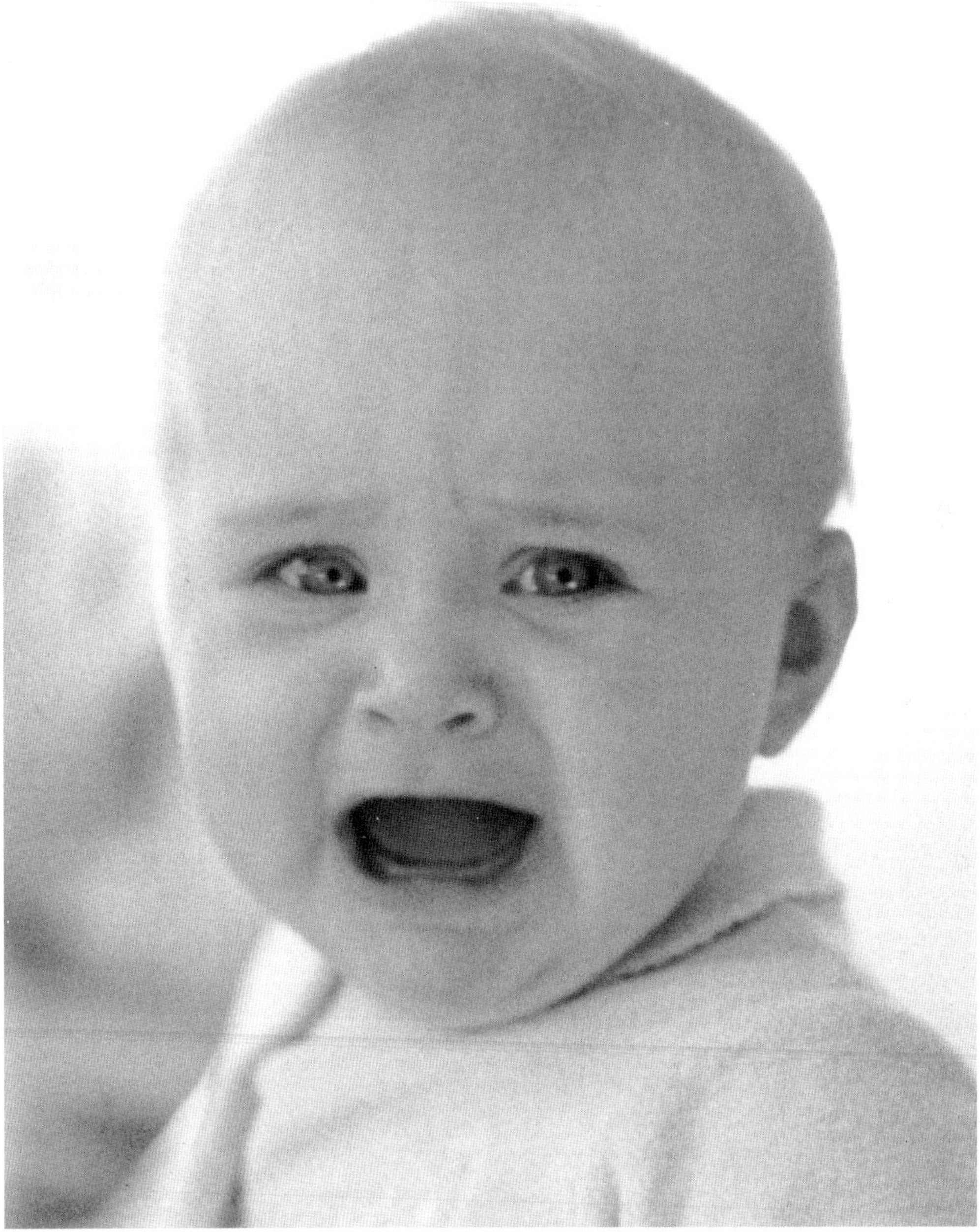

CRYING

Before your baby can talk or even grunt or point, her main method of communicating her needs is crying. One of the skills you learn as you get to know your baby is understanding the meaning of her various cries. The most common reasons for a baby to cry are fatigue and hunger. This sounds obvious, but in the commotion of the first months of life, sometimes you forget that it's been three hours since the baby started her last meal or that she's been awake for two hours straight. So feed her if you think she's hungry and let her go to sleep if you think she's tired.

After hunger and fatigue there are many reasons why a baby might cry. Maybe she has indigestion, maybe she's too hot or too cold, maybe she's feeling overwhelmed by life outside the womb. There are probably as many reasons for a baby to cry as there are feelings and desires for the rest of us. The best you can do as a parent is to *try* to understand and look for patterns with your baby, all the while reassuring her and yourself that she's safe and loved and you're doing your best. As time goes by and your baby adjusts to life and you get to know her and her needs, the crying will lessen.

MAKING A *PAKJE*

Oma's first response to a crying baby under three months is swaddling, or making a *pakje* (pronounced "pock-ya"). Literally, *pakje* means "little package." Very snug swaddling can be very comforting to a newborn. Oma doesn't know of one baby who has not been calmed by being made into a *pakje*. Many babies prefer to be *pakjes* at least occasionally or for sleeping. Newborns have no control over their limbs and they probably feel strange flailing around the way they do. Swaddling may remind them of being in the womb. It may make them feel secure. It is a good first solution to try for a baby who is crying.

There is a very specific way to make a *pakje*:

- ☐ Make sure baby has on a clean diaper and a clean undershirt.
- ☐ Lay a blanket on the bed or soft surface.
- ☐ Fold over the top corner of the blanket and lay baby down on it, on her side, arms folded in front, head on the folded corner.
- ☐ Fold the corner of the blanket closest to you over baby and tuck behind her back.
- ☐ Lift up the bottom corner of the blanket and tuck it behind baby's back.
- ☐ Wrap the last corner of the blanket around baby and pick up the *pakje*.

Pakjes are much easier for relatives to handle (see "Visitors" chapter), and they're easier to feed also. Oma always wraps a *pakje* on alternating sides to remind the mother which side she should start nursing on next and also to alternate on which side she puts a *pakje* down to sleep.

As your baby gets older you can loosen the *pakje*. As she gains control of her arms, leave them out but still give her firm support around her tummy and legs.

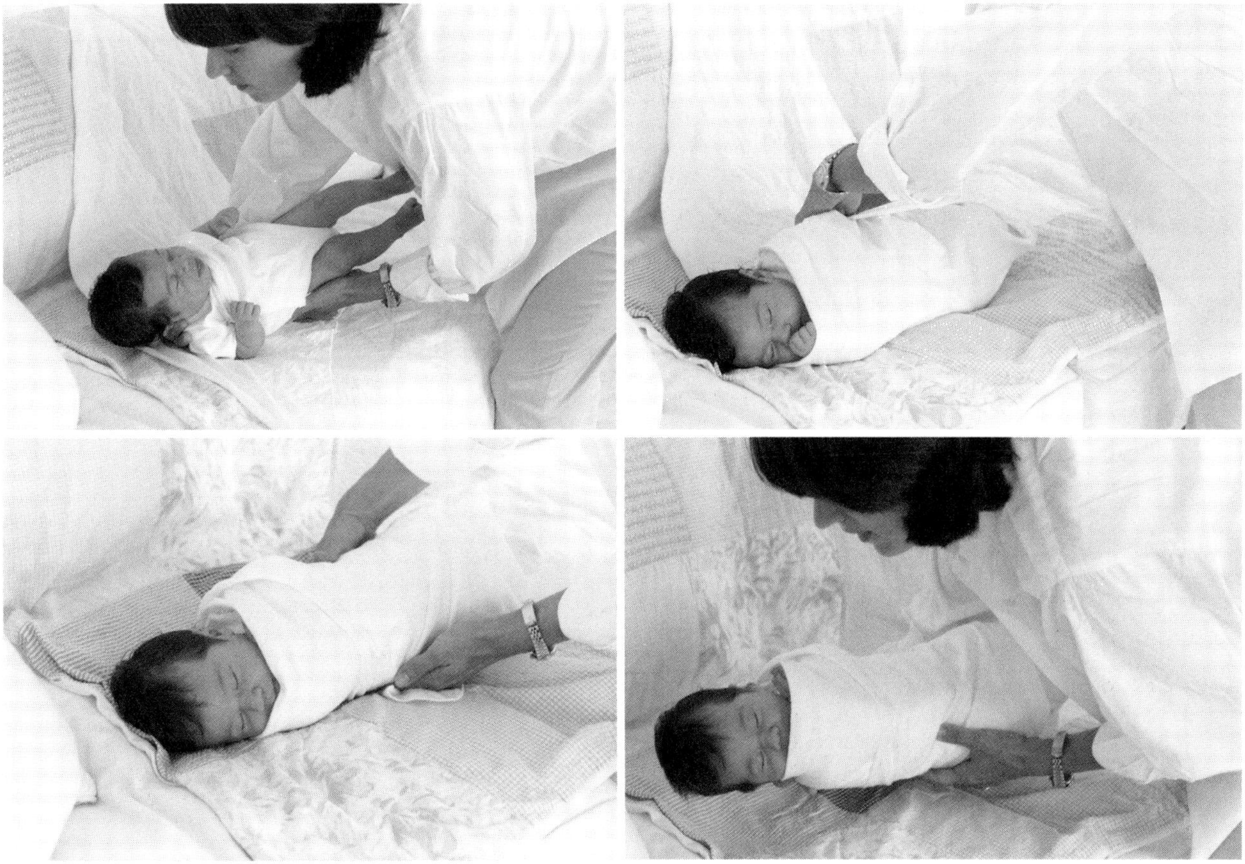

OTHER REASONS YOUR BABY MIGHT BE CRYING

If your baby continues to cry, take a look and listen around. Is it very bright? Noisy? Too dim? Too quiet and boring? Sometimes a radical change of scene helps. If you're inside, go outside; if you're outside, go inside. Your baby can sense when you get frustrated, so change your plan of action. Sometimes just the change of pace, air, or light makes all the difference to both of you.

If she is having trouble digesting, some light pressure against her tummy might make her feel better. A tight *pakje* can provide support for her tummy against the pressure she's feeling from inside. Try holding her in your arms with your breast pressing against her tummy and gently pat her back. You can also hold her up against your shoulder and pat her back. Make sure you have a burp pad over your shoulder when you do this in case the troublesome gas and milk comes out. Another way to provide light pressure for your baby's tummy is to lay her flat, tummy down, across your legs or on a firm bed and gently pat her back. Or let her lie face up on your lap with her head near your knees and move her legs in a bicycle motion.

Oma has noticed with many babies that the act of sucking can actually help a baby's digestion. Let your baby suck on a pacifier occasionally after a meal to help with digestion.

COLICKY CRYING

Some babies cry only when they're tired, hungry, have gas, are overstimulated, or bored. Once you get to know these babies you do what they need you to do. You feed them, you play, you put them down in their crib. You feel masterful, proud. You're good parents, after all, because you've learned your baby's signals and your baby usually doesn't cry for more than a few minutes.

The answer to some babies' crying is not so simple. Maybe they cry all evening and into the night. Maybe they cry after eating. You feel bad, tired, incompetent, and if you're nursing, downright sour. Everyone looks at you as if you don't know what you're doing. Everyone offers advice and criticism. You're tired, you feel alone. It's really hard. And exhausting.

First of all, you have to rule out illness. This is difficult, and you and your spouse should be thorough. Discuss your concerns in detail with your pediatrician. Once you've ruled out illness you need to take turns taking care of the baby. If you're nursing,

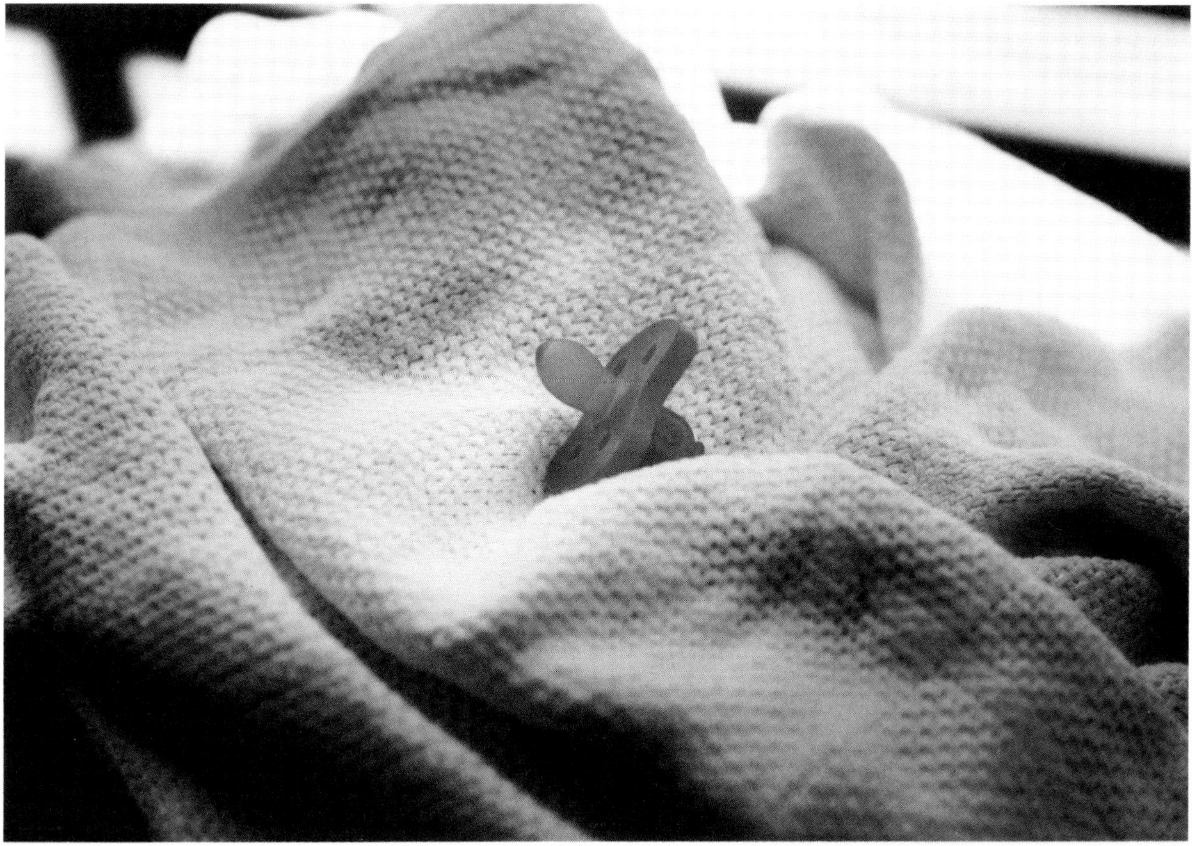

ask your husband to take a walk with the baby while you rest. If your husband is up with your crying baby at night, you go to sleep. If you're up, tell him to go to sleep.

You also need to try to keep a constructive attitude. One way to do this is to try to see things from your baby's perspective. Oma is a master at this. You can imagine your baby may be having trouble digesting, or maybe she's having trouble adjusting to life outside the womb in some other way. Maybe she needs to cry as physical exercise because she doesn't know how to move her limbs on purpose yet.

Oma suggests that if nothing but walking around with her against your shoulder helps, then make sure you use good posture and make exercise out of it. Turn on some music and get up a good pace, even if it's just three steps forward, turn, and three steps back. Tuck your pelvis under you and hold her with your arms, not your lower back. Think about how strong you'll be when it's all over. You and your husband can take turns at this brilliant exercise.

Finally, try everything that everyone suggests, and then try everything in reverse order. When you're finished, maybe she will have outgrown the crying. Above all, keep trying to learn what your baby likes and doesn't like, but don't worry yourself too much over it. The excessive crying will pass in anywhere from two weeks to four months.

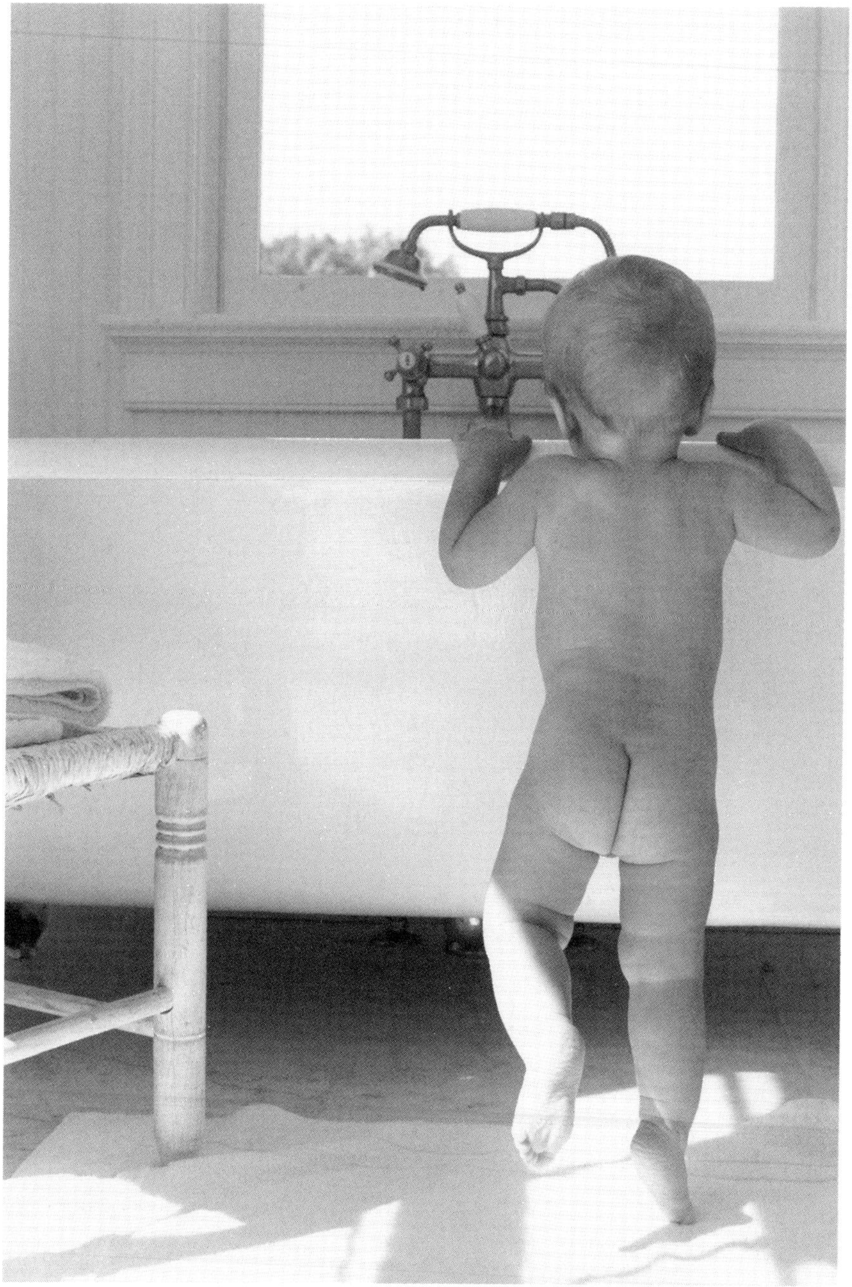

BATH

Splashes and giggles, blowing bubbles and singing. Most of us remember loving bath time, and we want our babies to love it too. But babies are small, slippery, and delicate, and there are a few things you need to know about bathing them. Once you learn how to be prepared and your baby is a few weeks old, you'll be on the road to giggles.

First of all, Oma advises: Don't do it alone for the first few weeks. Your baby isn't jumping in mud puddles or smearing peanut butter in his hair yet, so it's okay if you wait to bathe him until your spouse or a capable friend or family member is around. It's great to have someone to grab an extra diaper or hand you the shampoo or take the baby in a dry towel when you're finished, or even to take over the bath halfway through when your strength gives way. Don't underestimate how much energy it takes at the beginning, especially when you've just been through childbirth. The first few times I bathed our first baby I had to quit two minutes into it, shaking and sweating.

Also, don't expect to answer the door or the phone while bathing your baby. Even if you have a curved changing pad and you *think* your baby is nowhere near being able to roll over, there are many ways he could end up on the floor. If you need to look away from him or reach for something, always put one hand firmly on his stomach to hold him in place. If you must step away from the table or bathtub, just pick him up in the towel and take him with you. In an emergency, placing him on the floor is better than leaving him on the table or in the bath.

HOW OFTEN TO BATHE YOUR BABY

Take the cue for how often to bathe your baby from your baby's skin. A baby with dry skin should be given a full bath only two times a week, as long as you clean his bottom and neck well each day. A baby who sweats a lot or has supple skin can handle more-frequent baths. If you can't settle on a bathing schedule, talk it over with your pediatrician.

WHEN TO BATHE YOUR BABY

There are many good times during the day to give your baby a bath. You should do it when the time is right for both of you. For a baby who enjoys a bath it works as good exercise before a last feeding and sleep. But if a bath excites your baby or irritates him, it would be better to bathe him in the morning only, when you and he are more rested and less irritable. A bath with sunlight pouring in the window can be magical. A bath can be given for lots of reasons: to soothe, to clean, to distract, to postpone, to cool off. It was a revelation to me when Oma told me that baths can be used as an activity, not just as a chore for the end of the day.

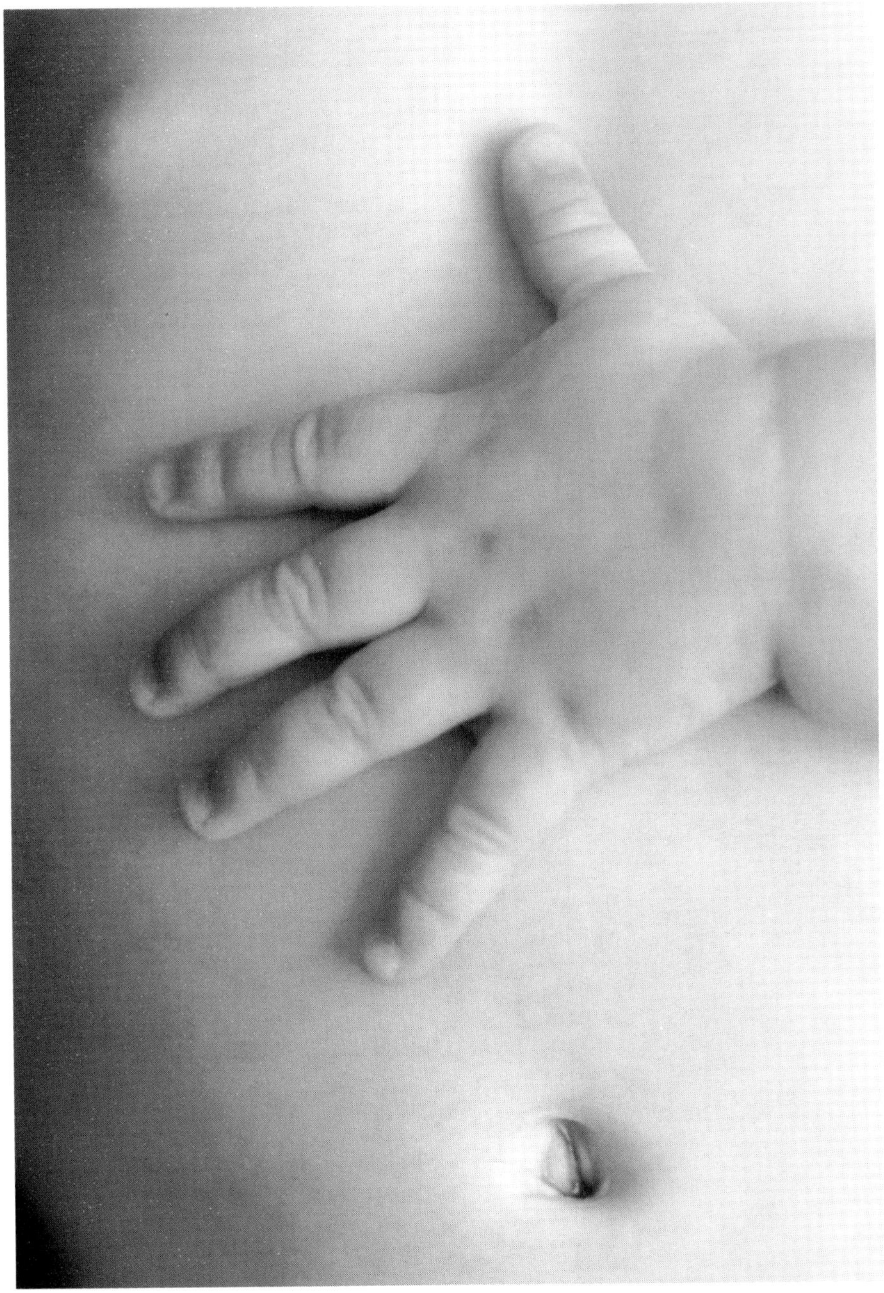

You need the following to bathe your baby:

- ☐ Changing table (before the umbilical cord heals)
- ☐ Clean kitchen sink or baby bathtub (after cord heals)
- ☐ Big bath towel, folded in half on the table as an absorbent cushion
- ☐ Two thin baby washcloths, one for washing, one for rinsing
- ☐ Bowl of clean, quite warm water
- ☐ Thin, hooded baby towel
- ☐ Baby shampoo, to be used sparingly
- ☐ Baby soap, to be used sparingly
- ☐ Two clean diapers, because babies have a way of pooping if you have only one
- ☐ Clean outfit, including knit cap

Oma is very strict about white towels. You don't want any dyes to get on your baby's skin, and you want to know when it's clean or not. You can wash white towels in hot water to kill any bacteria, and you should rinse them an extra time to make sure all of the detergent gets out. This being said, if you receive a blue towel with beautiful eyelet trim as a gift , use it with no remorse.

HOW TO GIVE A WASHCLOTH BATH

Until your baby's umbilical cord dries up and falls off, you should not submerge his body in water. He needs a washcloth bath. I recommend a washcloth because you can launder a washcloth much more easily than a sponge, and you can get into all the little folds of the skin with a washcloth, which you can't do with a sponge.

The best place to give a washcloth bath is on the changing table. You'll have diapers and ointment, rubbing alcohol to clean the umbilical cord, cotton balls and clean clothes handy, and you will already have placed the changing table out of any drafts. Before you get him undressed make sure the room is warm.

As with everything else having to do with taking care of your baby, being prepared before you start is everything, so get together and lay out everything you need before you undress your baby. Then wash your hands.

When everything is ready:

- ☐ Undress your baby.
- ☐ Wipe his bottom if necessary.
- ☐ Cover his lower half with a corner of the big towel.

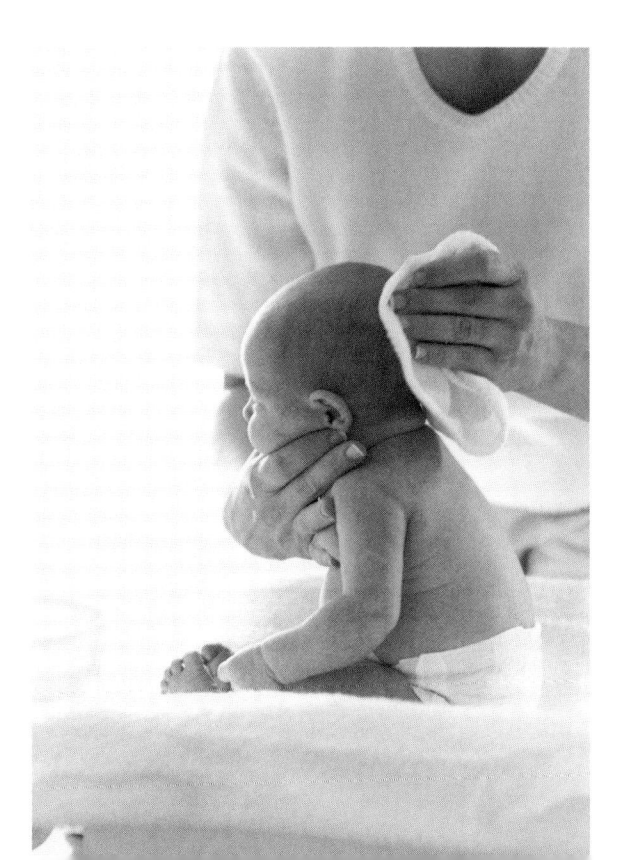

Babies have trouble maintaining a good temperature, so have only half of your baby's skin exposed at a time.

When cleaning your baby you want to move from the cleanest, most delicate part of the body to the most soiled, so that you don't spread any germs. This means:

- Start with your baby's eyes, very gently.
- Then wash his nose, head, behind his ears, neck, under his arms, and his hands.

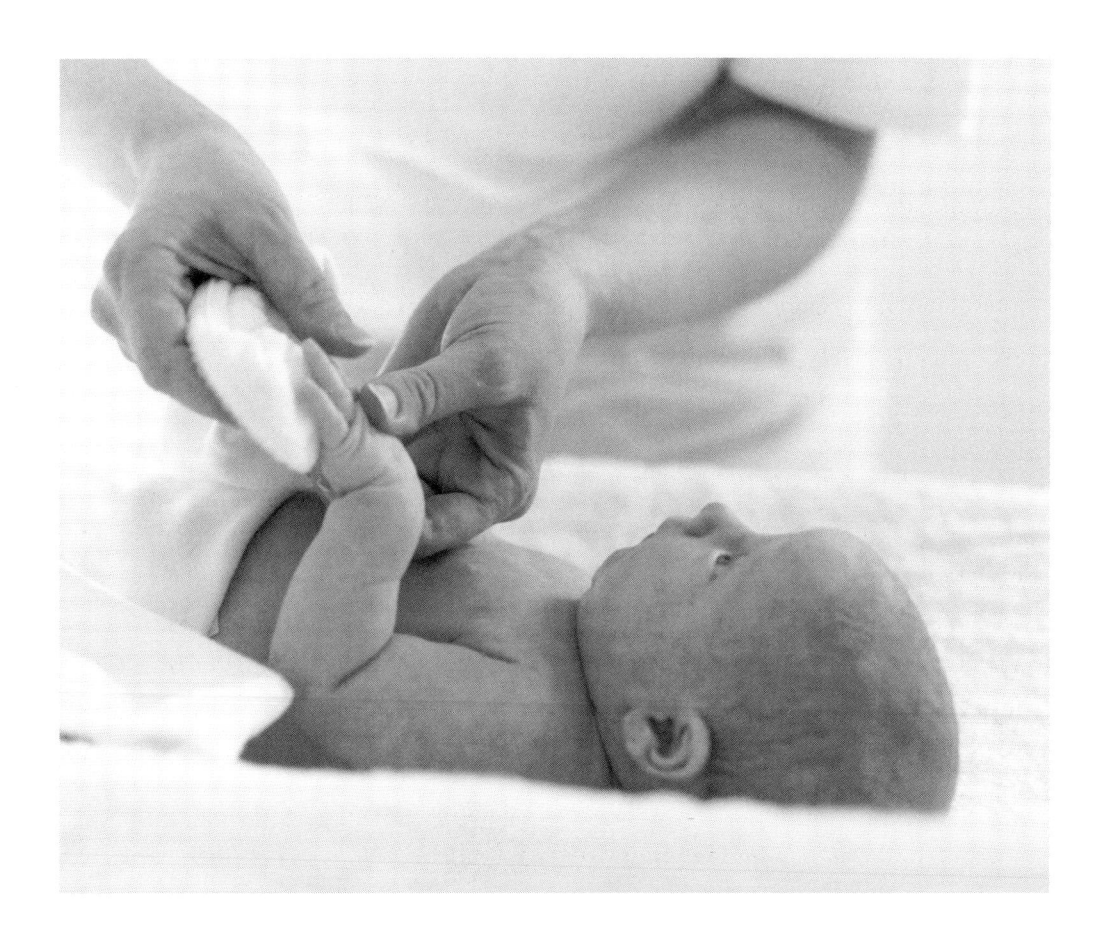

Make sure you get into all the folds of the neck and behind his ears. To clean the back of your baby's head, sit him up and let him lean forward, holding him firmly by the jaw. Make sure you clean between all of his little fingers to get any lint out, but Oma also likes this because it stimulates circulation.

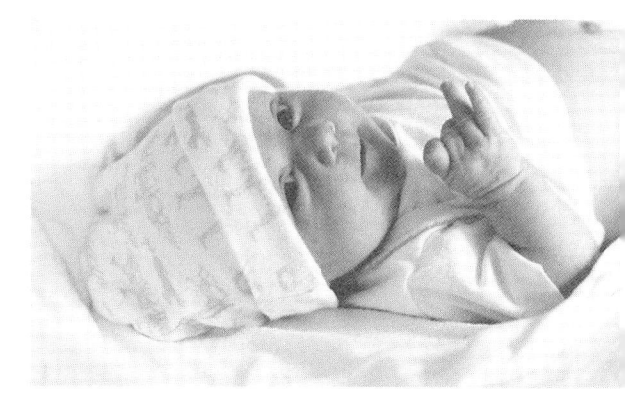

- ☐ Dry his head and upper body.
- ☐ Put on an undershirt and light knit cap.

Once the upper body is clean and dry and dressed, you can clean the lower body. This means:

- ☐ Clean the umbilical cord with alcohol to help it dry up.
- ☐ Clean between all of the toes and in the folds of the legs.
- ☐ Clean gently in the folds of the penis or labia.
- ☐ Lastly, clean the bottom well with a touch of mild soap, making sure to rinse thoroughly.

Also:

- ☐ Make sure you dry in all the folds of skin you washed.

Oma recommends blowing gently between your baby's fingers and toes to dry them. Babies love this.

After a washcloth bath is a good time to let your baby go diaperless for a few minutes if the room is warm enough. It's good for his skin to breathe for a little while before going back into a diaper. If he's in a good mood let him lie on the dry towel and kick and reach without the restriction of a diaper. Try putting him on his tummy and letting him try to lift his head. Then:

- ☐ Put on a diaper and dress his lower body.

HOW TO GIVE A SINK OR TUB BATH

Once your baby's belly button is healed, you can submerge his body in water, which means you can give him a tub bath. Some babies love this development. They stay warmer, and the sound and feel of the water can be fun. But a lot of babies prefer to stick with a washcloth bath for a while. Don't force the issue. Wet babies are very slippery, and *you* may want to stick with a washcloth bath for a while also. Take your cue from your baby and your own strength.

The kitchen sink, if it's big enough, is the best place to give a baby a bath, because there you don't have to bend over or kneel for a long time. Whatever place you use—kitchen sink, baby bath in sink, or baby bath in big tub—it should be clean, out of a draft, and there should be a secure flat surface right next to it.

Oma reminds you, as with a washcloth bath, it is critical that you have everything you need for a tub or sink bath ready ahead of time, opened and laid out, so that you're not rushing around with a wet baby looking for things.

Oma also strongly recommends putting a hot-water bottle folded up in the clean clothes and towel before bathing. This way, by the time the baby comes out everything will be toasty for dressing. All of Oma's babies had this for every bath. If you want to heat up your baby's clothes in the dryer, just be careful that any snaps aren't still hot when you begin dressing him.

Once everything is laid out and ready, follow these steps:

- ☐ Double-check the temperature of the water with your elbow.
- ☐ Undress your baby and give his bottom a wipe if necessary.
- ☐ Lower him into the bath with both hands, one hand with a firm grip behind the lower back of the head, the other under the bottom.

When bathing your baby in a tub, follow the same routine you used for a washcloth bath:

- ☐ Begin with washing the eyes.
- ☐ Wash the head, neck, underarms, and hands.
- ☐ Wash the feet, legs, tummy, penis and scrotum or labia.
- ☐ Finish with the bottom.

The most important things you can do to make a sink or tub bath a comfortable experience for you both is to keep a firm hold on the back of your baby's head so that he cannot slip away from you, maintain eye contact with him the entire time, and smile at him. It sounds a little silly, but even if you're really unsure of yourself and nervous, a plastered-on fake smile will fool your baby and make him feel at ease. I was amazed the first time I actually followed this advice of Oma's. It really works. You might think your baby is smarter than that, but if his only physical feel of you is a firm hold on the back of his head (and this is very important), then your expression is all he has to go on. He can't feel your heart beating when he's in the water.

Another thing you can do to make your baby's bath more comfortable for him is to keep one wet, warm washcloth on his chest at all times, and clean him with the other. Then alternate the cloths for the rest of the bath. It may sound complicated, but if you have a firm hold on his head with one hand, then your free hand can easily do the rest.

When you're finished cleaning your baby:

- ☐ Lift him out of the bath with both hands.
- ☐ Lay him down on the baby towel.
- ☐ Slip the hood over his head.
- ☐ Dry in all the folds of skin that you washed, again blowing between his fingers and toes.

As with after a washcloth bath, this is a good time to let your baby stretch and kick with no diaper if it's not too cool in the house. Just spread a towel on the floor and play for a bit.

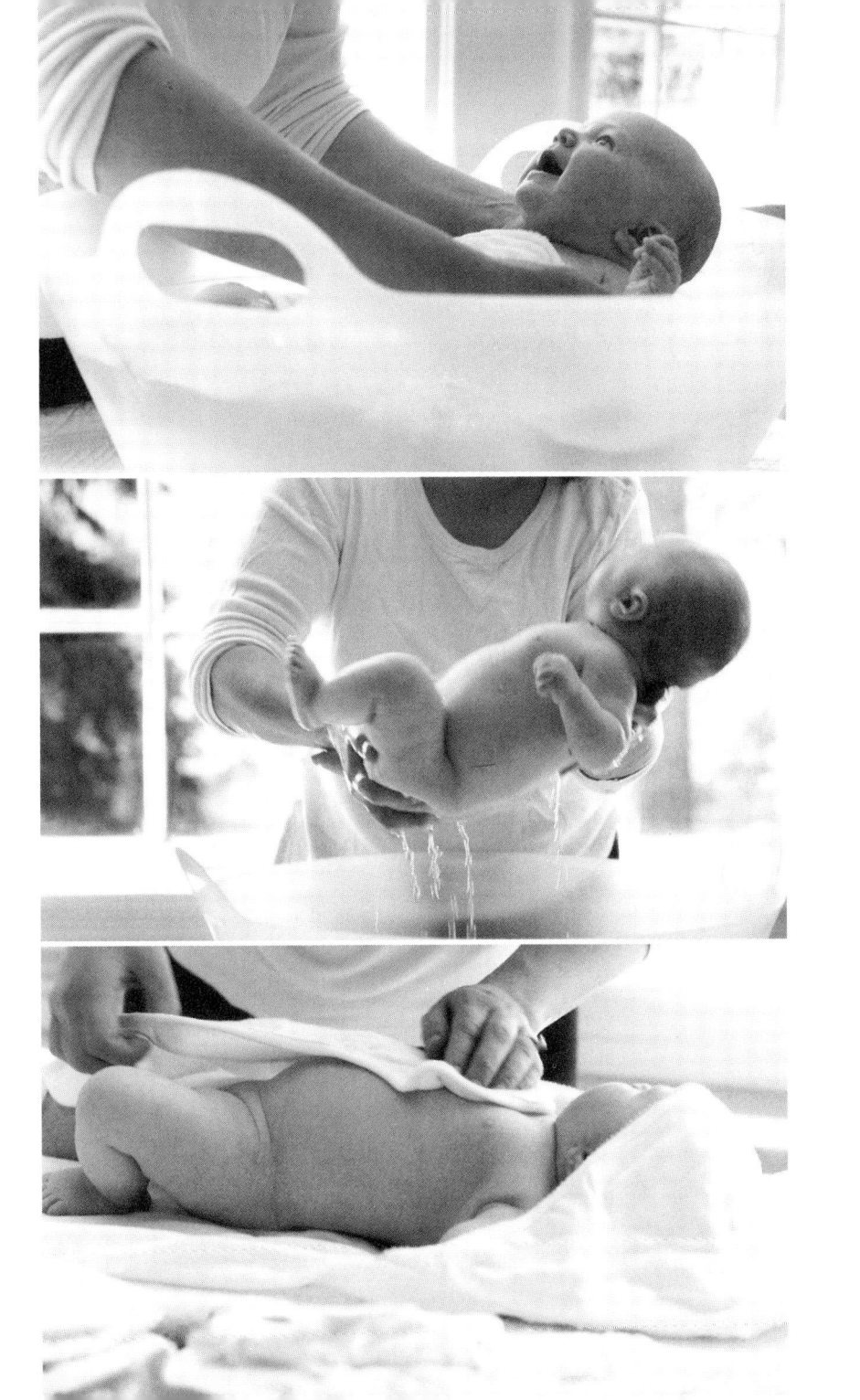

BATH

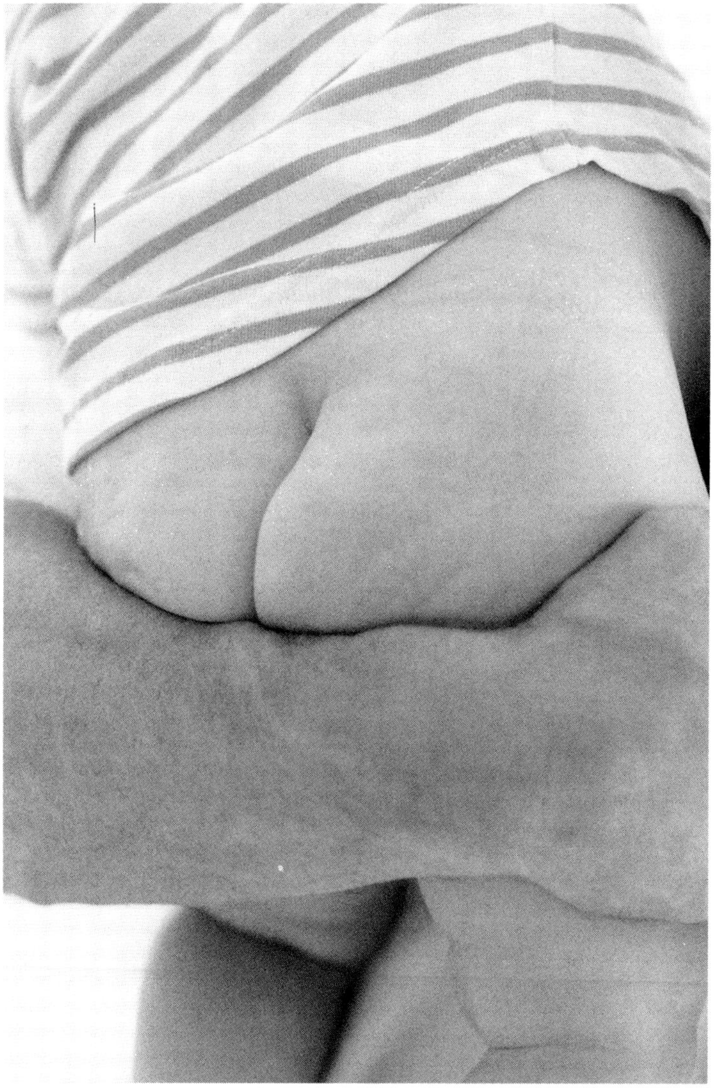

DIAPER

Diaper changing, like a lot of baby care, can be seen as a chore or as an opportunity. Since you'll be doing it eight to ten times a day, you may as well enjoy it. As Oma would say, once you get the hang of it, changing a diaper is something your hands do while you're talking and playing with your baby.

Make your changing table a nice place. Hang an unbreakable mirror next to where your baby will be lying, have some rattles and teethers handy. Have plenty of supplies. Most of all, if you live in a house with more than one level, have a changing place on every level.

Diaper changing can also be a handy way to get rid of guests who are overstaying their welcome. Few people like to watch the proceedings (see the "Visitors" chapter).

This is what you'll need to have on or near your changing table:

- ☐ Lots of diapers, disposable or cloth or both
- ☐ A spray bottle with water, wipes, or both
- ☐ A box of strong facial tissues or cotton balls or both
- ☐ Zinc-based ointment (Desitin, Balmex)
- ☐ Petrolatum-based ointment (Vaseline, A&D Ointment)
- ☐ Cornstarch baby powder, to be used in moderation and carefully

Oma fills up the spray bottle with warm water before the diaper change. There are also wraparound warmers available in catalogs.

Ointments are good if your baby has developed a rash, because they protect the skin from further irritation. Oma suggests you change ointments occasionally or alternate their use so that any chemicals in a particular ointment don't become irritating to the skin.

Cornstarch powder is useful in hot weather or if chafing is a problem, but use it very sparingly so that it won't clump when it gets wet. It's also very important to be careful not to let the powder get into the baby's lungs. If you want to use it, pour (don't shake) some powder into your hand below the level of your baby's head and near the foot, not the head, of the changing table. Then smooth the powder onto her bottom and in the creases of her legs. Don't shake powder directly onto your baby's bottom, because her bottom is too near her mouth and nose and she might breathe it in. The safest thing to do is not to use powder at all, but rather let your baby's bottom be bare in fresh air as often as possible in warm weather.

HOW TO CHANGE A DIAPER

Before I say anything else, Oma reminds me to tell you that whenever you need to reach for anything or even look away while your baby is on a surface above the floor, you must keep one hand firmly on her stomach to hold her in place. Even when they're very young, babies can arch their backs and squirm off a surface.

When you're ready lay your baby on the changing pad face up and do the following:

- ☐ Unfasten the soiled diaper and leave it under the baby's bottom.
- ☐ Hold your baby's legs up by the ankles with one hand.
- ☐ Spray the labia or penis and scrotum and bottom clean, into the soiled diaper, with the other hand.
- ☐ Pat the bottom dry with a tissue or cotton balls.
- ☐ Put the tissue in the soiled diaper and replace the soiled diaper with a fresh diaper.
- ☐ Apply ointment or cornstarch powder if necessary.
- ☐ Fasten the new diaper.

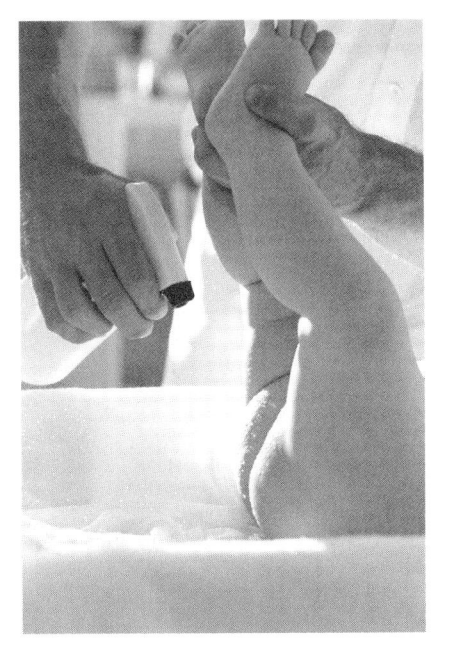

You may see other people using wipes at home, but plain water is much more gentle to your baby's skin. A well-respected pediatrician I know suggests to his patients that they wash their hands with wipes instead of soap and water for a day to see how it makes their skin feel. I'll tell you now to spare you: They're really drying and foamy. Water works well to clean a bottom, and you'll help avoid diaper rash by not breaking down the skin with all of the chemicals and rubbing. A few sprays of the water bottle and you avoid a lot of wiping of delicate skin. Wipes are convenient sometimes and they're necessary when you're away from home, so do have some on hand, but use the spray bottle at home.

My husband's and my favorite way to clean a very messy bottom is to hold a baby or child over the sink by letting her lean forward over your forearm, in a sitting position, and wash the bottom with a warm, clean stream of water with the other hand. If you spread your baby's legs on the edge of the sink and dip his or her bottom down a bit, you can rinse the labia or scrotum (not to mention the upper thighs) much more thoroughly than with wipes. We do this for as long as a child is in diapers. We have two stacks of towels in the bathroom: one stack of hand towels and one stack of "bottom towels" for whoever is in diapers at the time. You may raise a few eyebrows washing your babies' bottoms this way, and Oma never did it, but your babies will have comfy, non-chafed, clean bottoms all day.

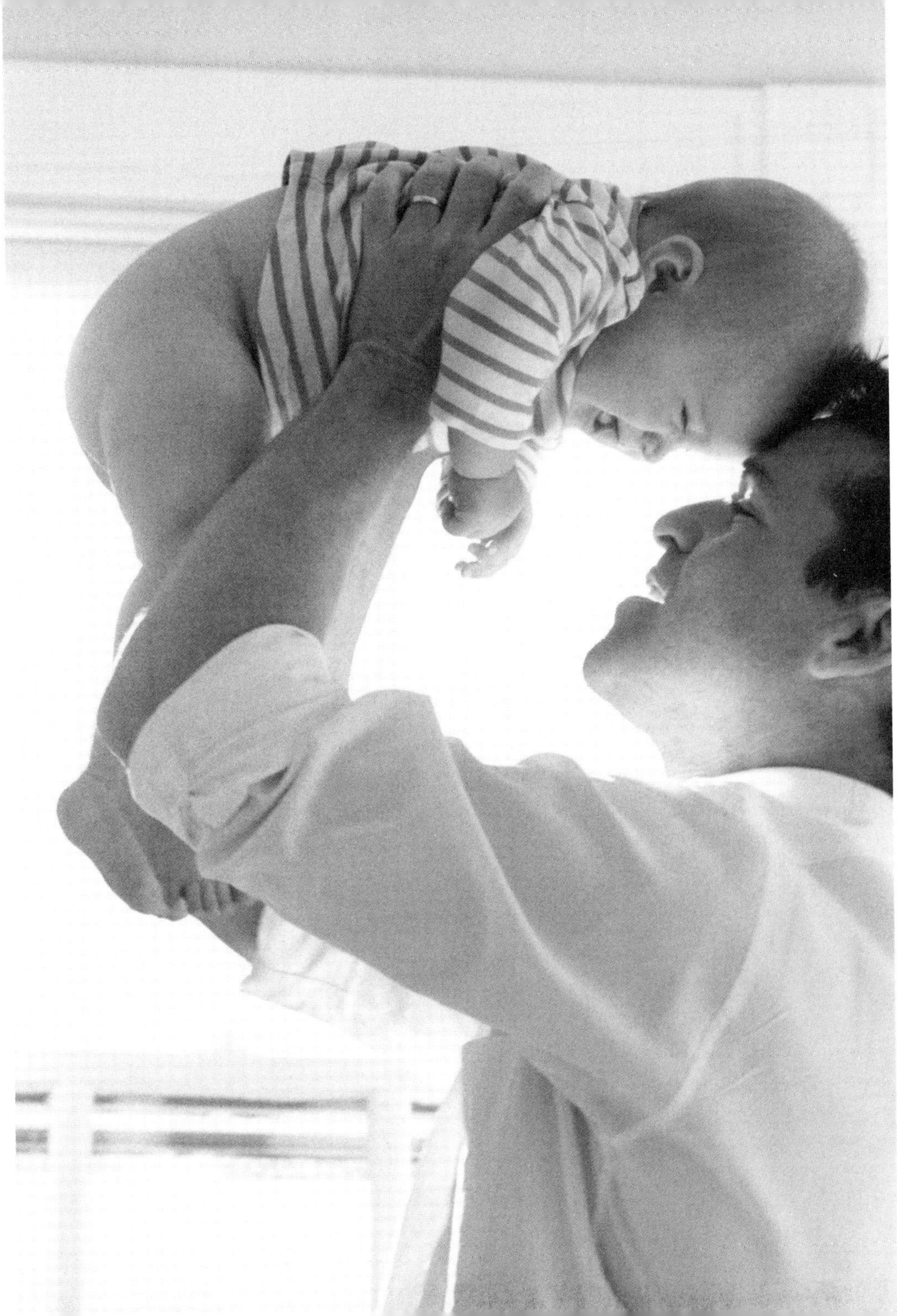

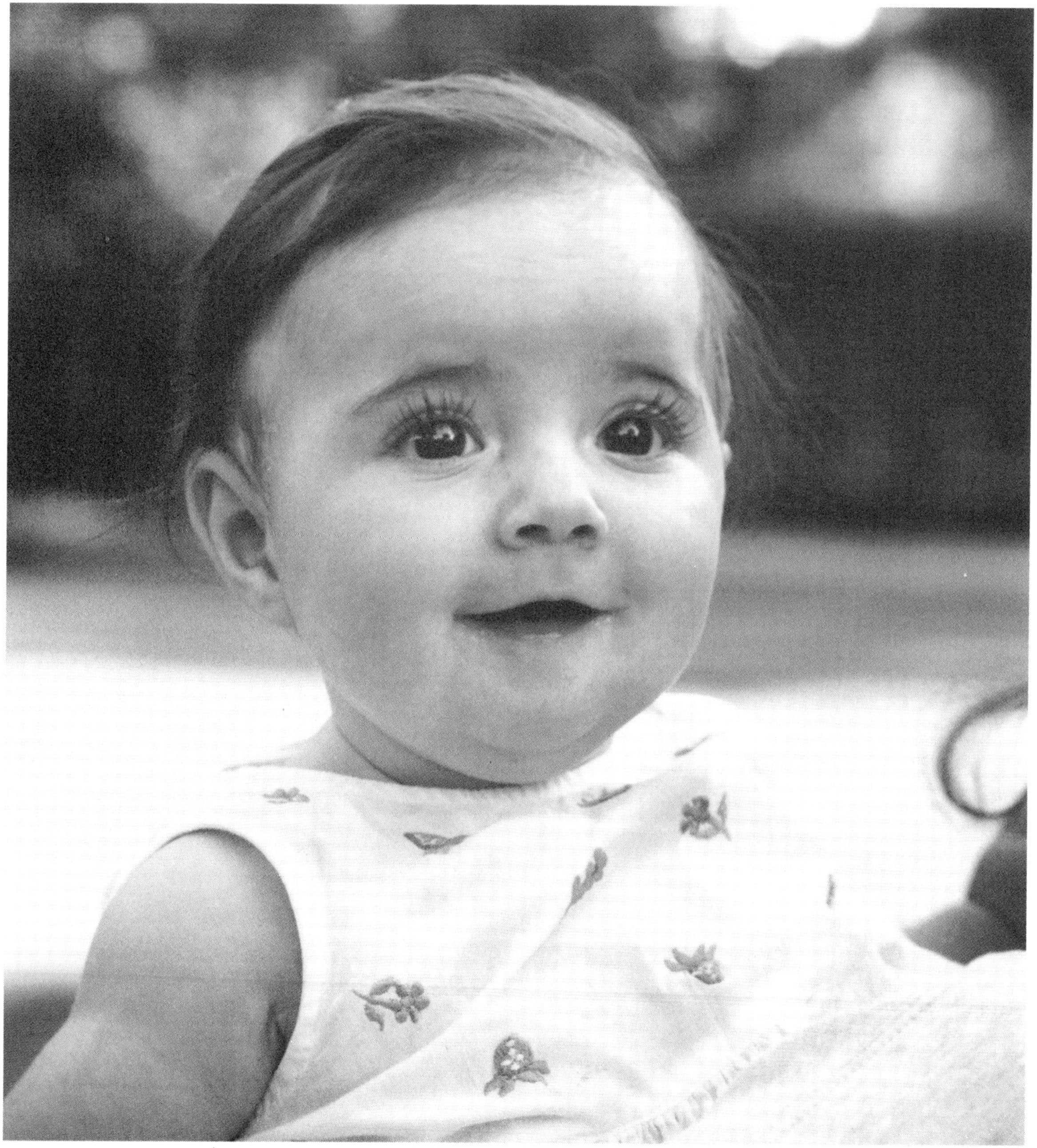

PLAY

When thinking about play for your baby, remember that the whole world is shocking and new for him. He has never seen, smelled, touched, heard, or tasted in the outside world before. The littlest things are fascinating or upsetting. Recognizing a pattern of light and dark, learning the smell of his father, hearing a doorbell for the first time are all new adventures. From your baby's point of view there are five areas of play: sight, sound, smell, touch, and taste.

Try to introduce new sensations to your baby gradually so that he can absorb them in his own way and not feel overwhelmed. Your baby's first experiences will lay the foundation for his sense of security and understanding, so take your time with him and try to see the world from his perspective while gently expanding his horizons.

SIGHT

Visual play for a baby is based initially on seeing the difference between light and dark, seeing the difference between movement and stillness, and recognizing a face. These are all very important skills for a baby to learn so that he can see when his environment changes and recognize who is a known person and who is a stranger. With these ideas in mind there are many toys you can make and games you can play.

The best visual game of all for you and your baby is when you sit with your knees up and let him sit in your lap and lie back against your legs. In that position, face to face, he can see your face at close range, see your eyes blink and your mouth move, learn the color of your hair and your skin. Very soon after birth your baby will recognize your face as distinct from any other. He sees your arms reach and your hands with fingers moving and your face with smiles and a nose that sticks out when you look sideways. He will learn to look into your eyes and hold your gaze for longer and longer.

Related to this game is Oma's strongly recommended practice of taking your baby everywhere around the house with you. Put him in an infant seat, in a front carrier, or securely prop him in a stroller and do what you need to do around the house, but bring him with you. He'll see sheets flying, shower curtains opening and closing, dishes shining and moving one after another out of the dishwasher. He'll pass by light windows and dark doorways, all the while trying to keep track of that familiar shape that is you. He'll learn about space, light, and relatedness. As long as you keep moving he'll probably keep being interested, and you'll get the housework done while you're at it.

Black-and-white mobiles are good for babies to look at also. Your baby will be able to focus on the moving parts if the mobile is hung about eight to twelve inches from his face. You can mount a mobile on a stroller, an infant seat, or the side of a playpen or crib, and the gentle movement will be quite interesting. Patterned fabrics also hold interest for babies. Try laying him down next to a richly patterned pillow.

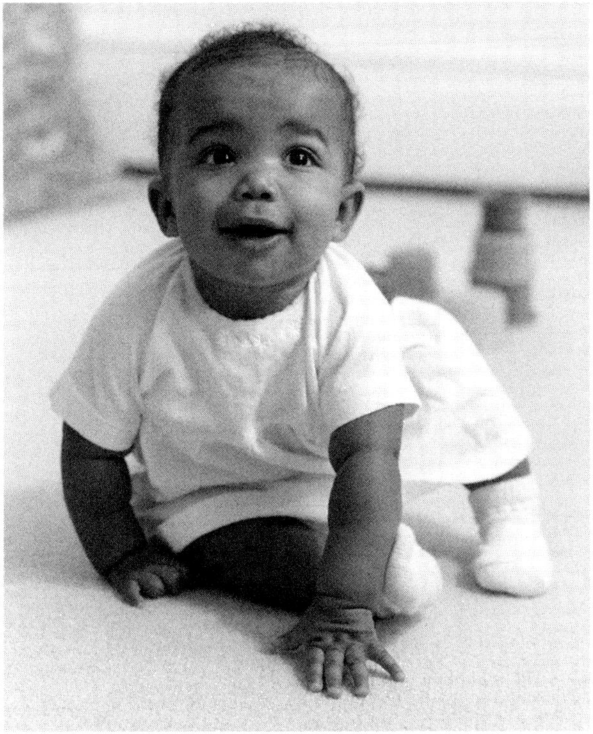

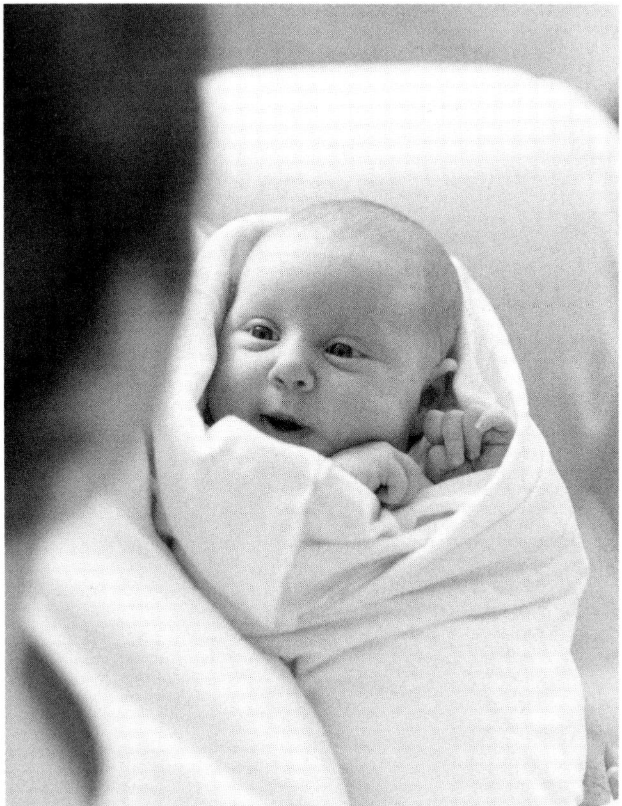

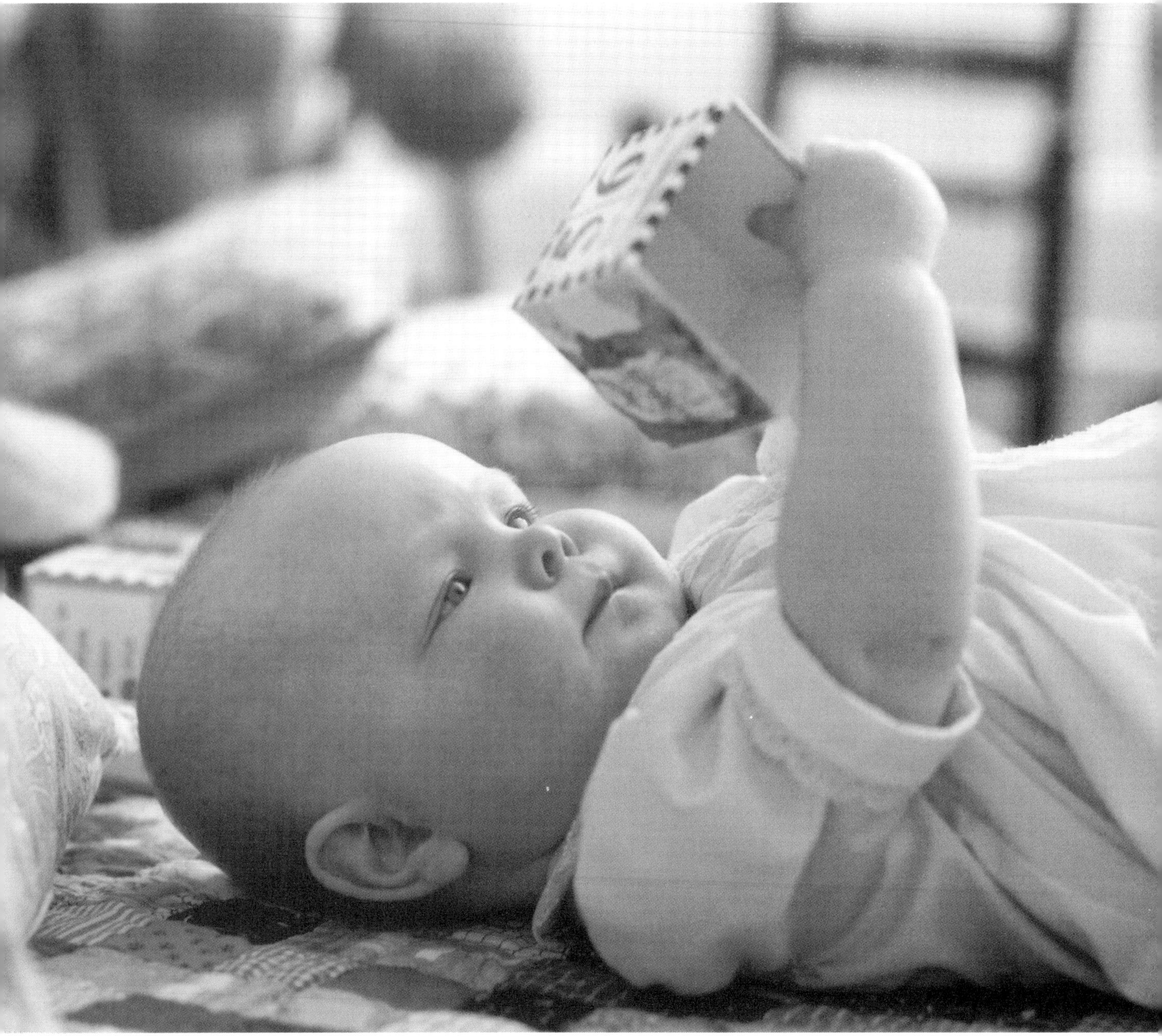

Take your baby outside and explore the world when he's awake and alert. The branch of a tree swaying in a breeze with fluttering leaves is fascinating. A trip to a grocery store is an adventure to another world.

Once your baby can sit up and hold on to things, you can set him up on a quilt on the floor anywhere. He'll be able to see all around him and pick things up to inspect them. Give him plenty to explore, two or three at a time: wooden spoons of different sizes and weights and textures, a set of measuring spoons, a plastic cup, a toy with a face, a clean hairbrush, a whisk. Let him see and feel everything that's safe, keeping in mind that everything you give your baby will end up being sucked on and chewed.

Oma suggests having a basket of clean, safe "toys" for your baby in every room along with a blanket or quilt for the floor, so that you always have a safe and interesting place close at hand at a moment's notice.

Once your baby is several months old he'll be able to see color, and it's fun to replace some of the black-and-white toys with brightly colored toys and mobiles. Look around each room every week or so for new objects to explore.

SOUND

Sound play is based on learning your voice and hearing and learning the meaning of other sounds.

An integral part of Oma's important take-along-everywhere-in-the-house game is talking to your baby as you go. Tell him everything you're doing and he'll hear what your voice sounds like close up, at a distance, when you're complaining, when you're joking. He'll hear a window opening, a door closing, water running, your footsteps, and the ringing of the telephone. All these sounds will register with your baby in some basic way as familiar. These sounds will add up to "home."

You can also slowly introduce him to other people's voices and animal sounds at a farm or zoo. The more slowly you introduce new sounds, the more your baby will be able to distinguish between them and make sense of them. Of course, this process will occur whether you guide it or not, but if you're aware of the process you can have fun with it and avoid overwhelming him.

Oma listens to every sound a baby makes as a great effort on the baby's part to communicate. Early on you can take your baby's "ooohh" as a special message of love or response to a question and reply to him, keeping eye contact, and waiting for another effort. You can engage a baby as young as a few weeks old this way, and in a few months you'll be having full-fledged baby "discussions," which will lay the foundation for a relationship between you of understanding and communication. By the time your baby actually speaks recognizable words, you'll already be understanding his meaning and he'll already be confident that you're listening.

Also treat your baby to music. Simple rhymes and melodies will introduce your baby to your language and culture. Harmony and the flow of a song will make an impression on him. See which of your music he seems to like. Make music a part of your day by singing and listening while doing other things. Soon your baby will associate certain music with certain activities, he'll calm down and go to sleep when he hears some music and rev up and expect an outing when he hears other music.

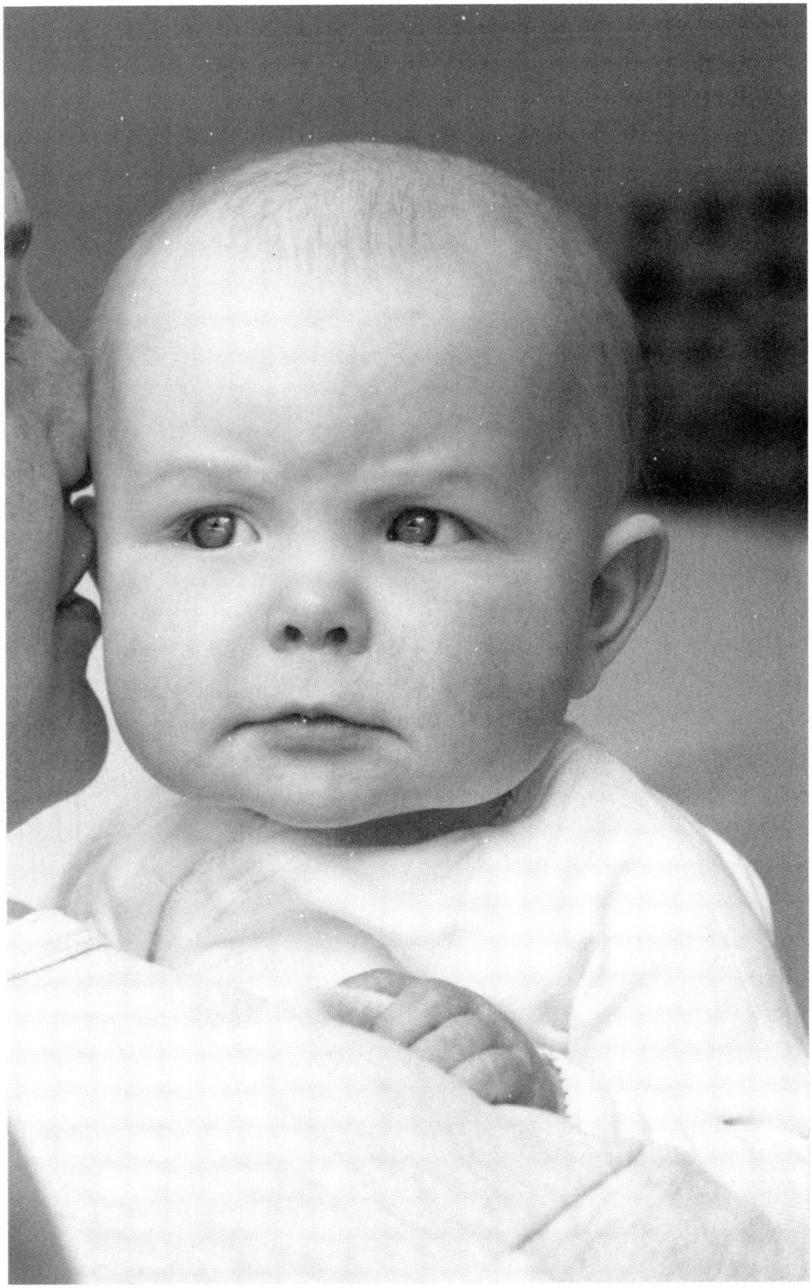

SMELL

To your baby there are two smells: you and everything else. Smells probably associated with you are your breath, breast milk and/or formula, a warm stretchy blanket, your bed, his bed, and probably a few other things and places around the house. Smells that are foreign and therefore probably a little interesting and a little scary are other people's breath and body smells, unfamiliar food cooking, car exhaust, and detergent, to name only a few. Even the sensation of smelling is new for your baby, and when added to too many other new sensations at the same time, it can be distressing.

Oma recommends trying to be aware of what smells you expose your baby to, not so much to limit them but rather to better understand what reactions your baby might have to the smells. Is he soothed by the smell of your favorite meal? Does he look around for Grandma when he smells fresh air blown in through the open door?

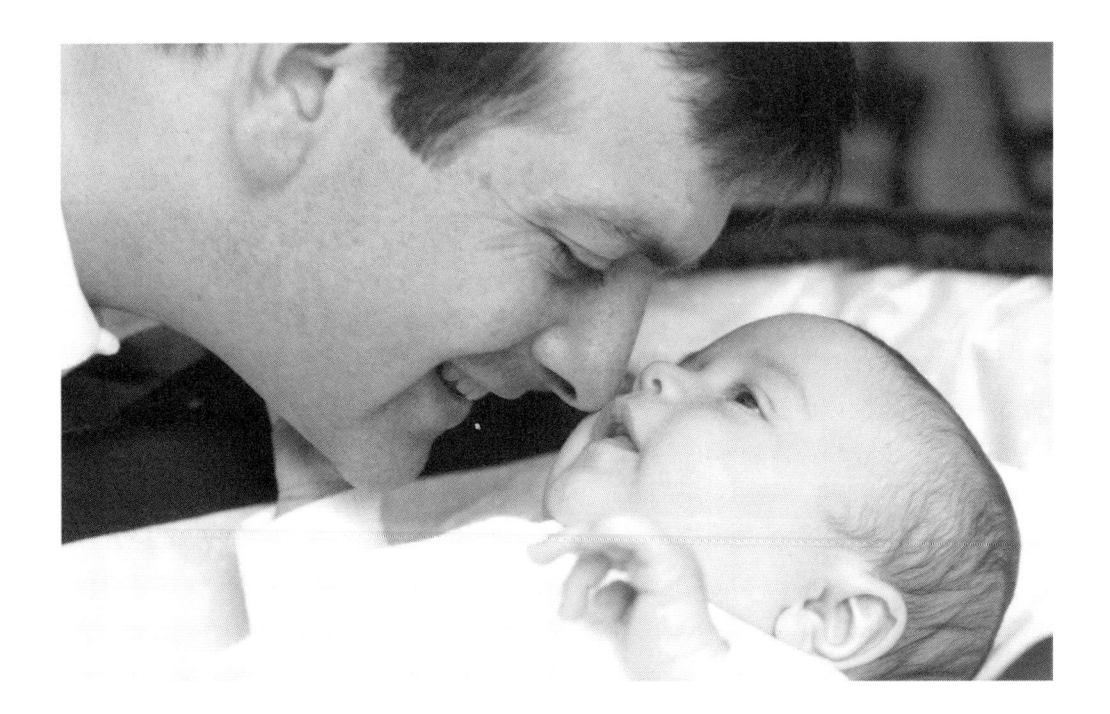

TOUCH

Your baby's experience of touch is made up of his touching things and also being touched, or handled, by you and others. He learns a lot about you from how you handle him. Every diaper change, every time you hold him to feed him, bathe him, kiss him, every time you nudge him to make sure he's secure in his baby seat, he learns that he is valued, taken care of, loved.

Up to about six weeks old babies probably aren't able to sense their bodies very much, especially their extremities, unless they are touched. So if you massage your baby's fingers and toes he might begin to sense that he *has* fingers and toes. If you rub his legs with lotion, stretching his muscles for him, he might make a first effort at trying to stretch himself on purpose.

You can lay the foundation for physical awareness for your baby right from the start by touching him and holding him and taking care of him gently and firmly. He will learn your touch—just as he learns your face, voice, and smell—as being confident and loving, and that will be the cornerstone of his life experience.

Once your baby is able to reach out and pick things up and touch them himself, you can introduce him to an array of textures and shapes with toys and household items as described in the section on "Sight." A fluffy lambskin, a soft worn blanket, whiskers on Papa's face, a cool breeze, silky grass—these can all be delightful touch experiences. Pay attention to how he reacts to these things, and talk about them and react to them with him. How funny is it to have your hair blown up around you by a gust of wind? How surprising is it to feel the prickles of a hairbrush for the first time? How overwhelmingly lovely is it to feel your baby's cheek against your own? All of these experiences are what make up the kind of "play" for your baby in which he can really participate.

Once your baby can roll over, sit up, and crawl, you can play games using your own body as a jungle gym. Make a bridge for him to crawl under by getting on your hands and knees. Make a bar for him to pull up on by holding your opposite elbows. Make your legs into a slide. Learn yoga or a calisthenics routine, and your baby will love playing on and around you while you get your body back in shape.

TASTE

Related to smell is taste. To your baby there is milk/formula/you and then there is everything else: someone else's finger, a teething ring, the edge of a blanket. Your baby will learn over time how to distinguish among smells and tastes until, as a two-year-old or before, he'll ask for a bite of the candy you thought you were sneaking, and he'll notice the difference between brands of the same kind of cereal.

Once he can swallow solid food you can explore the worlds of vegetables and fruit, fish and meat, and grains (see "Food").

BABY-PROOFING

There are catalogs and stores full of products to help you lock up all your cabinets, your toilet, and your oven in defense against your exploring baby. The best and easiest way to baby-proof your home is to make your home baby-, child-, and adult-friendly. Make your home a place that is fun to explore and easy to be in. Two things you can't move are your stairs (get a gate) and your electrical outlets (get plugs). But for the rest, organize your home so that objects are placed at age-appropriate heights.

Pots and pans, plastic containers, dish towels, unopened containers of food, baby toys, wooden and washable upholstered furniture, clothing, and very heavy books go down low. Forks and knives, glassware, opened containers of food, telephones, magazines and newspapers, and *unplugged* kitchen appliances go at four-year-old height. Medications, detergents, very sharp knives and implements, expensive jewelry, important documents, and valuable breakables go high up in cabinets or on high shelves. Consult your pediatrician about your baby's growth curve when planning shelving and cabinets.

It may take longer to rearrange your possessions than to buy locks and install them, but once you're done you won't have to worry about the locks being left unlocked, you'll have to say "no" a lot less, and you'll have age-appropriate household items available for everyone's use.

As far as ovens, stoves, and toilets go, there is no substitute for careful use of these and supervision of your child. Turn the handles of a pot away from the edge of the stove, put your baby or toddler in a playpen, high chair, or on a designated rug before opening the oven; and keep the toilet lid down.

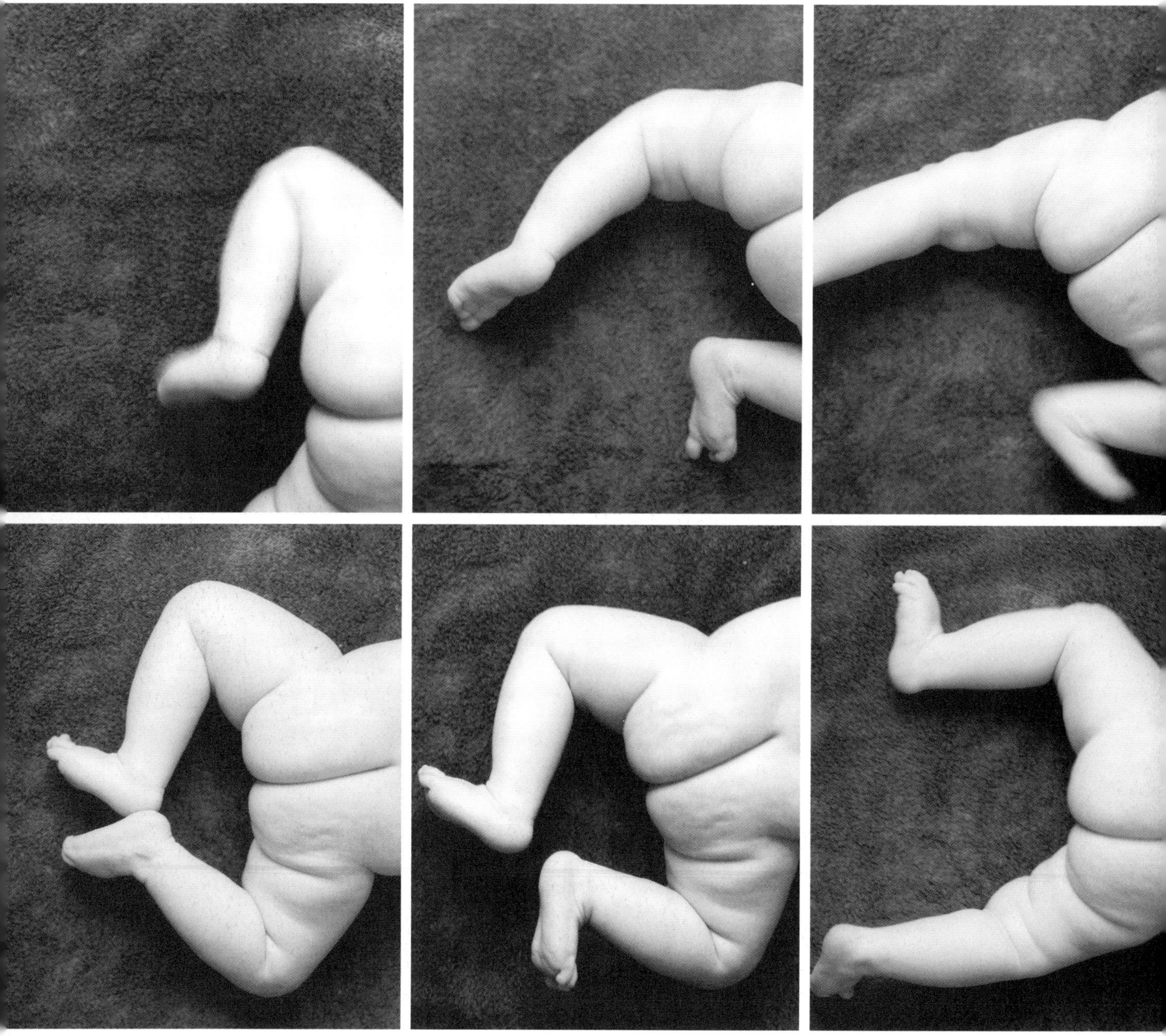

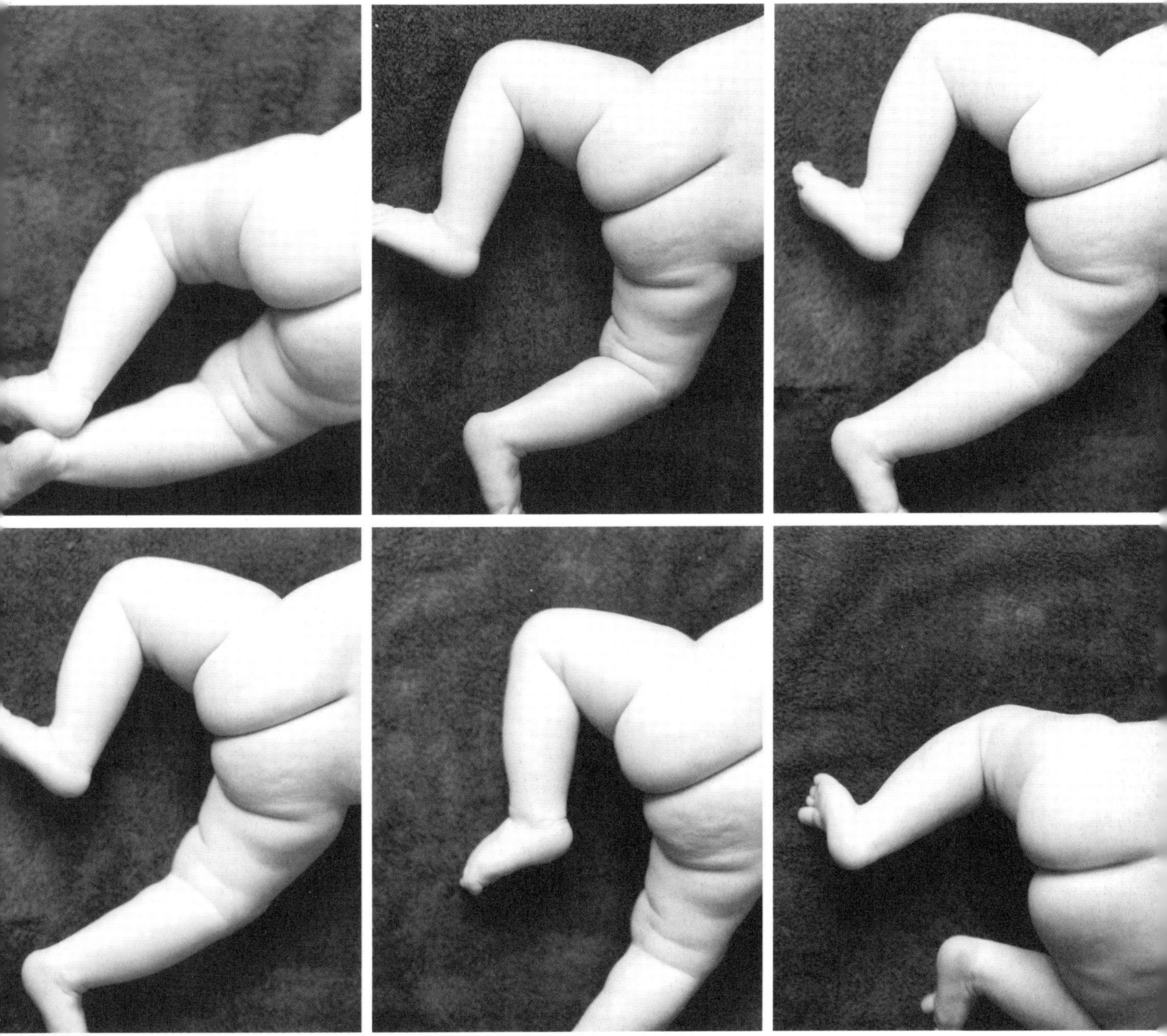

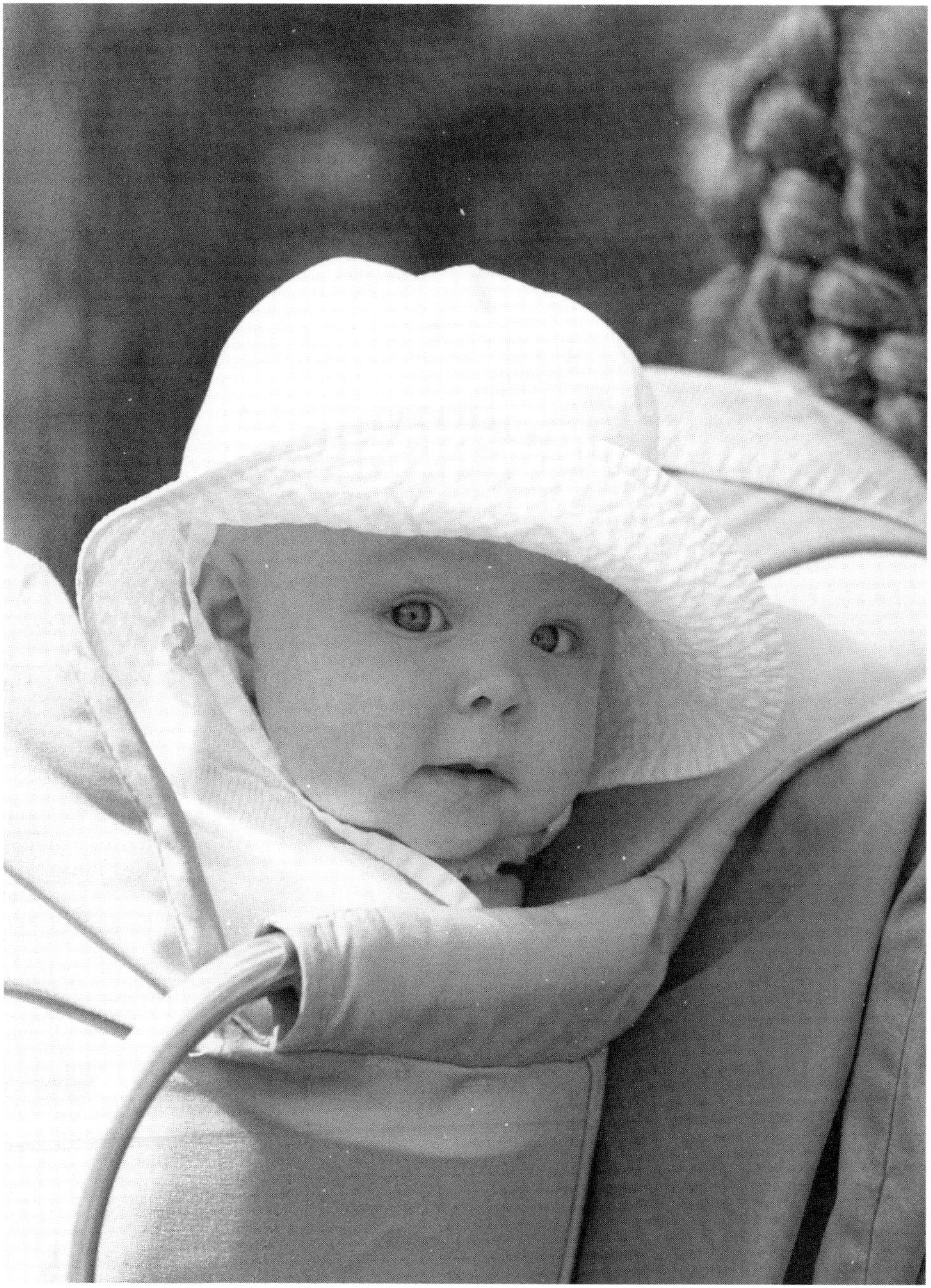

OUTINGS

When you first get home with your newborn baby, it's hard to imagine packing up to go do something, and for a few days you probably shouldn't. But sometime during your first week home you should get dressed, put shoes on, and go outside for a walk. It's good for your lungs, it's good for your muscles, it's good for your head, and it's good for your baby. Very soon, outings will become the focus of your day, and you and your baby will anticipate them eagerly.

TIMING AN OUTING

Oma's rule for new mothers is to plan to do one thing a day above and beyond the basic care of your baby. You will be able to do a lot in a day once she is three months old, but in the meantime you need to pick one thing a day and be satisfied if you almost complete that one thing. Taking one walk a day is a good way to start out.

At first you may be a bit shaky, so don't attempt to take a walk by yourself. Take a very short walk with your husband carrying his daughter or pushing a stroller at your side. Try it again the next day and see how you feel. The key is to not become exhausted but build up gradually until all of your strength is back.

It makes the most sense to make an outing when your baby is awake. That way when you get back you can feed her and both of you can take a nap. Also, when she is awake she will be able to start noticing the differences between outside and inside, the smells, sounds, and air outside (see "Play"). What you want to avoid is returning home tired when your baby has already had a nap.

OUTING EQUIPMENT

From the time your baby is born you'll want the following gear for outings:

- ☐ Car seat
- ☐ Stroller
- ☐ Front carrier and then frame backpack
- ☐ Diaper bag with changing pad

You must have a car seat for your baby even if you don't have a car. For the ride home from the hospital, for rides in taxis, for trips in friends' cars, for airplane rides, you must have an up-to-date, safe car seat in which to fasten your baby. Until she is twenty pounds the car seat must face the back of the car, and it should be in the center of the backseat. It's worth it to get a newborn car seat (for babies up to twenty pounds), because they fit a newborn better and so are safer than using a big car seat from the beginning.

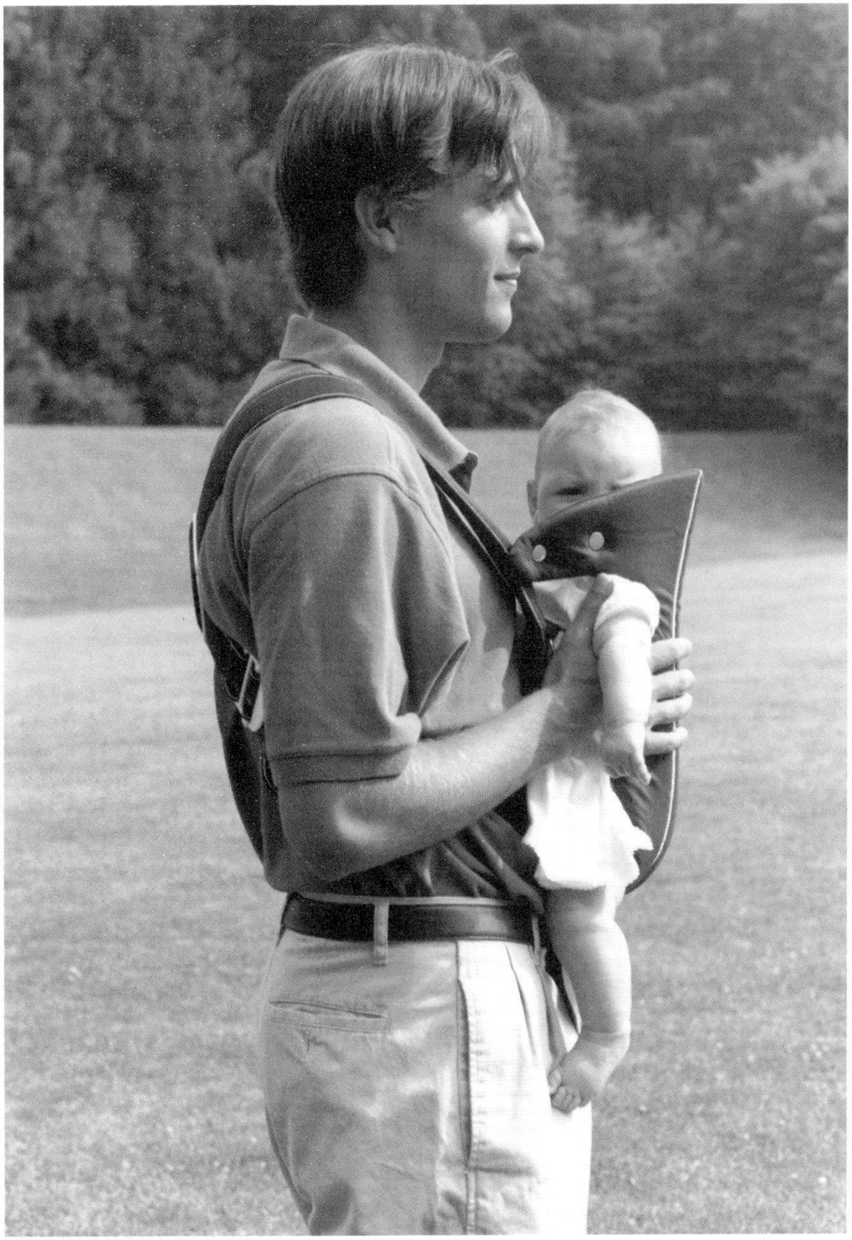

A stroller is a great device. You can walk with no strain on your back, your baby can lie down or sit up, and everyone is happy. For newborns it's good to have a flatbed stroller so they can stretch out while sleeping. From four months on, a sit-up stroller is recommended. If you plan to use your stroller mostly after driving somewhere, get the kind that can attach to the car seat so you don't have to transfer your baby when she's asleep. If you plan to walk a lot straight out of your door, get a sturdy pram with good, big wheels. You can buy any kind of stroller—from an old-fashioned pram with shock absorbers to a mini fold-up umbrella stroller—and you will use it all the time. Just make sure it's safe and has a good safety belt system.

Front carriers are wonderful for babies up to six months old, especially light babies, because you feel very mobile and your baby feels warm and close. Colicky babies love being strapped onto their father's chest for long walks. Many front carriers are constructed so that you can nurse while wearing them. Oma reminds you to wash front carriers frequently and rinse them well, because babies often suck and chew on them while you're walking.

Once your baby has good head control and can sit up on her own, you can start to use a frame backpack. Babies and children love the view from high up on your or your husband's back, and you can keep using it up to age three if your child isn't too heavy. If you have long hair make sure you tie it up or wear a cap to keep from having it pulled.

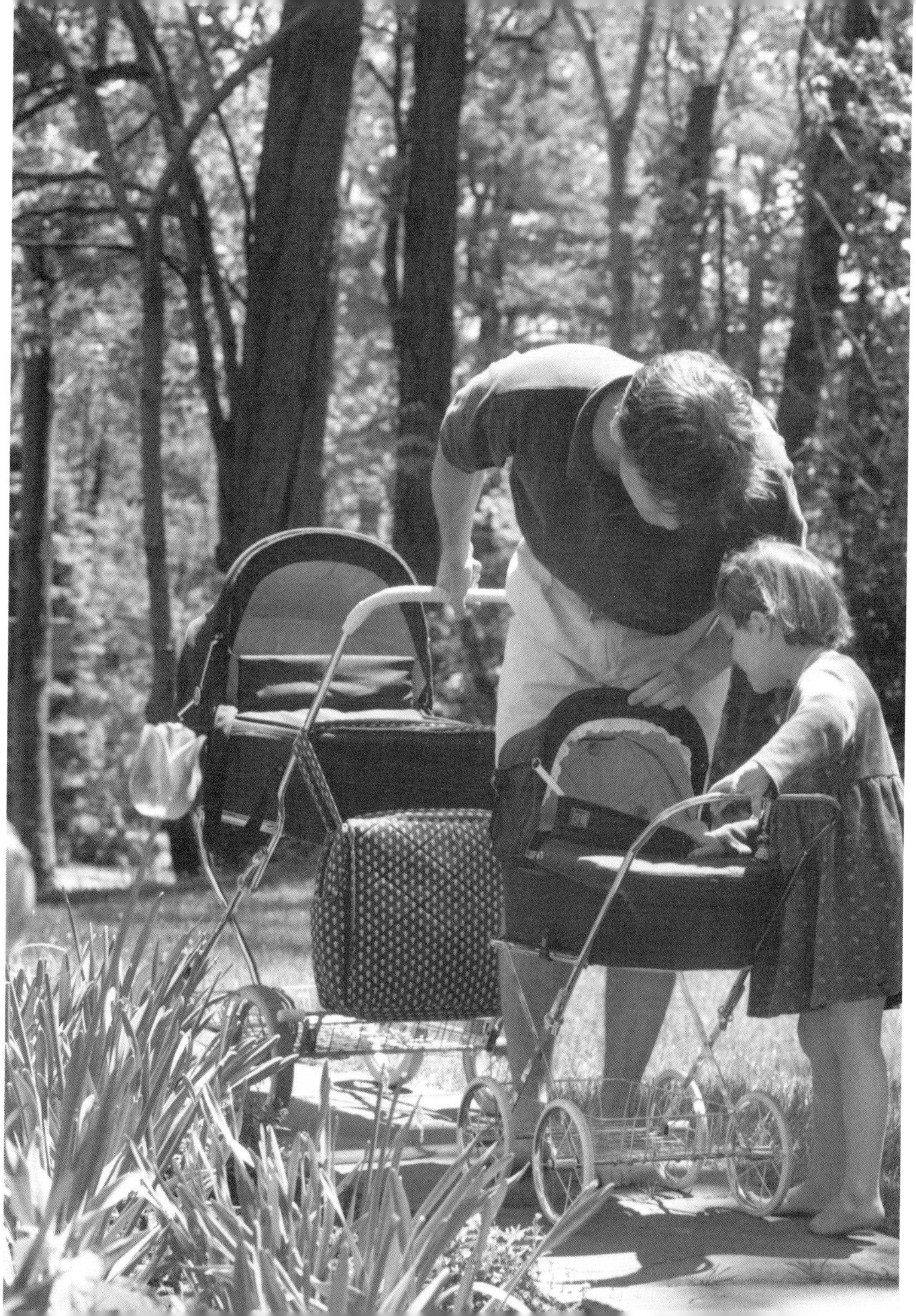

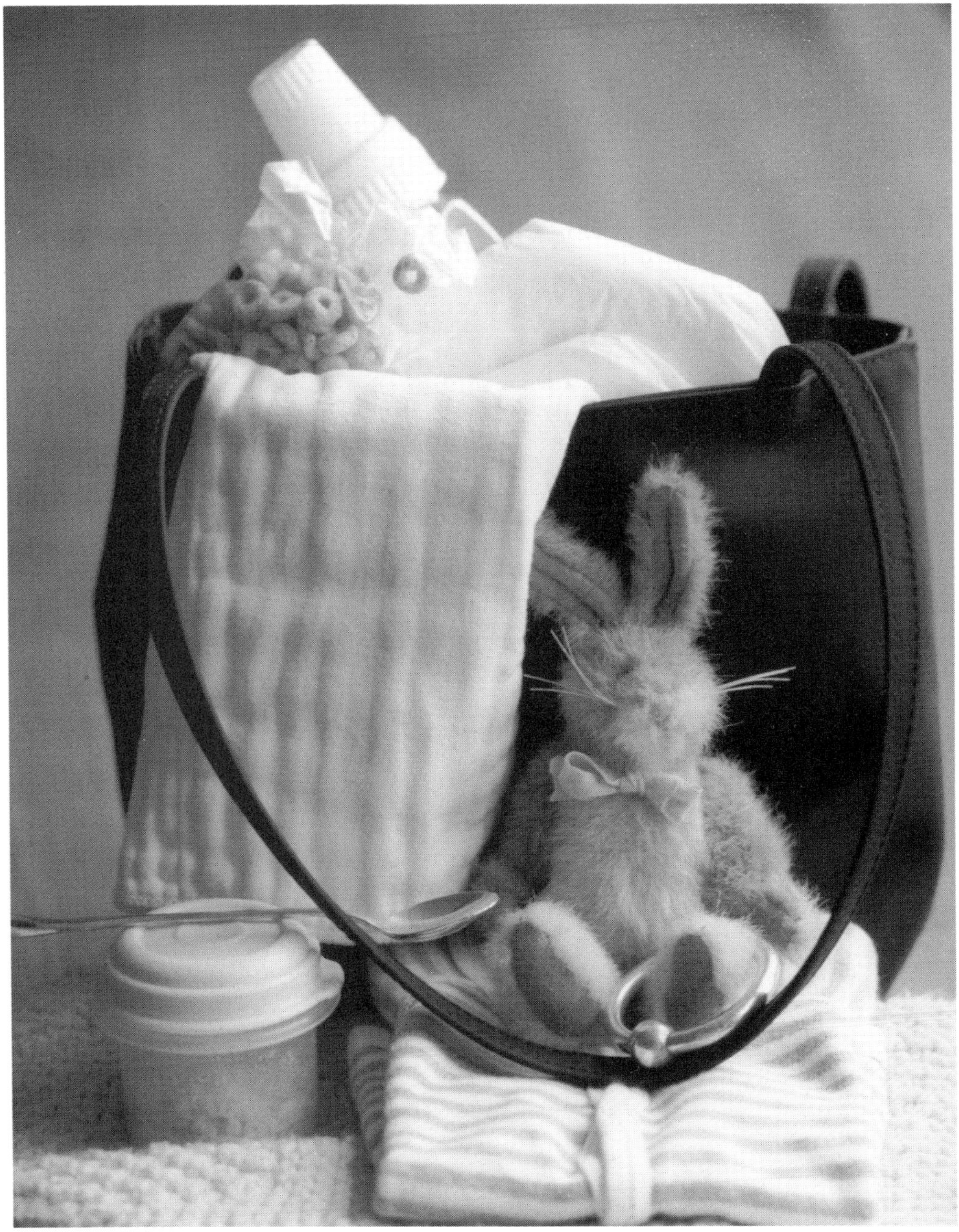

WHAT TO PACK IN THE DIAPER BAG

Once you have a baby you can forget about grabbing your keys and heading out the door. On the other hand, having a baby should not mean that you have to bring your whole life with you every time you go out. A huge bag will dampen your spirits and hurt your back. You can put everything you need for an outing in a manageable-size bag.

Whether you're going out in the car or walking with a stroller, or combining the two, you will always need the same things in your bag, so pack it once a season and replace items that you use when you get home again:

- ☐ Change of clothes
- ☐ Three diapers
- ☐ Small pack of wipes
- ☐ Next meal
- ☐ Water bottle
- ☐ Pacifier
- ☐ Two toys

This won't change until your child is four (except you'll skip the diapers and the water bottle will change to a water canteen), so get it straight now. Even if you're breast feeding, keep a can of ready-made formula and an empty bottle in the bag just in case. If all you have to do is grab the bag and your keys and slip your baby into a stroller or a front carrier, you'll be much more likely to go out on the spur of the moment than if you have to start from scratch.

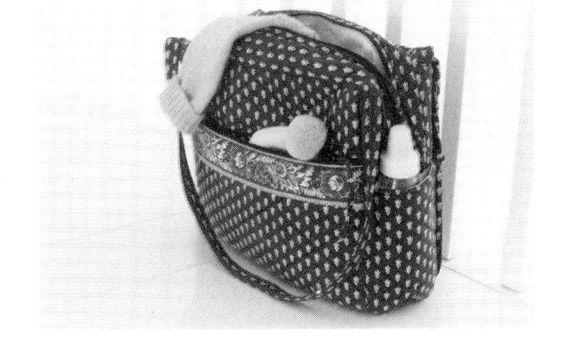

PACKING FOR OVERNIGHT TRIPS

The key to making overnight trips successful is not trying to recreate your whole home wherever you're going, but rather deciding what the most important elements of your baby's surroundings are and then figuring out how you can recreate just those. The two things that you'll probably want your baby to do predictably while you're away are eat and sleep. So bring her usual bottles and nipples, and bring her blanket and travel playpen. Bring two favorite toys. Beyond that, you're probably overdoing it. Don't underestimate how interesting it is for your baby just to be in a different place, and most places you'll go will have safe objects that you can use as toys. If you're less encumbered and more relaxed your baby will be too, and she'll get the idea intuitively that when you go away from home things are different, and that's okay and even fun.

The following is a good packing list for trips up to four days where there will be a washing machine and you will be able to buy diapers and food:

- ☐ Stroller or front carrier or backpack
- ☐ Travel playpen/crib
- ☐ Special blanket or stuffed animal
- ☐ Bottles, nipples, formula, if needed
- ☐ Collapsible booster seat with tray (six months or older)
- ☐ Two meals of cereal and baby vegetables
- ☐ Water bottle
- ☐ Four changes of clothes, three sets of pajamas
- ☐ Snowsuit or jacket, shoes or boots, and hats
- ☐ Two favorite toys

CAR TRIPS

Before you had a baby a car trip was a way of getting from one place to another. With a small baby, car trips remain almost the same, with a few nursing and diaper-change stops thrown in. Once your baby is about four months old and wants to roll over, sit up, and play, you've entered the era of car trips that take twice as long. You have to do the following:

- ☐ Forget about getting anywhere quickly.
- ☐ Become interested in every patch of grass, gas station, farm, fence, or field off the side of the road.
- ☐ Devise many finger and Velcro games, rhymes, and songs.
- ☐ Bring along snacks and a water bottle.
- ☐ Never let the car move without your baby buckled in her car seat.
- ☐ Feel very satisfied and contented if you drive for two hours straight.

AIRPLANE TRIPS

If you plan them well, airplane trips can be a breeze, because you can move around in an airplane. Do the following and you'll be on your way to enjoying flying with your baby:

- ☐ Encourage your baby to be very active before you board the plane.
- ☐ If your baby has colic, fly during a usually quiet time of her day.
- ☐ Save a meal or water bottle for takeoff and one for landing—sucking helps adjust ear pressure.
- ☐ For babies four months and older, bring snacks.

☐ Decide ahead of time not to let other people's comments and glaring looks get to you.

☐ Stick to your baby's schedule and change her into pajamas at bedtime, etc., so she doesn't think that the whole world is changing.

The more your baby feels that you're in control, the more secure she'll feel and the more normal she'll act. The best way to achieve this is to do what you would usually do, just do them on the airplane: take a walk, change her clothes, feed her, play. Bring something to read just in case she takes a nap, but don't expect it to happen. Wear clothes that you don't mind getting dirty.

UNASKED-FOR ADVICE FROM STRANGERS

A lot of people are very forward with comments and advice about other people's babies. Of course everyone has opinions about how other people do things, but when it comes to babies, people feel obliged to actually tell you what they're thinking, even if you haven't asked. Perhaps they believe they are the baby's only, if accidental, advocate. It begins with pregnancy and continues until your child is old enough to give a "who *are* you" look to the advice giver. In any event, you will develop an attitude toward this phenomenon, and it may as well be constructive. As long as you keep in mind that you are your baby's mother and that it's touching that other people care but that you don't really need to listen to them if you don't want to, you'll be operating from a nondefensive stance and you'll feel more in control.

You should probably listen to unasked-for advice as that person's advice about child care *in general*, not as a critique of your immediate situation. That way you can take it or leave it and evaluate it more objectively than you might otherwise. You know that your baby is hot and needs to cool off, but you might agree that in general babies should wear socks. You know that your baby's scalp needs sunshine because she's been inside for a day and a half and her hat's been off for a total of only three minutes, but yes, a lot of babies on the playground do have their hats on. You really don't need to justify your practices to total strangers. You are looking out for your baby's best interests as you see them, and that's all that matters. If your baby is crying because she's tired and you are rocking her to sleep and someone says to you, "She's hungry," don't start fussing around looking for a bottle or explaining that actually you think she's tired. Just smile and say, "Thank you." Of course, you are under no obligation even to acknowledge what people say to you in most situations.

On the other hand, you never know where you'll get the little tip that will make your life and your baby's easier or better, so do file the advice away somewhere in your head and review it later.

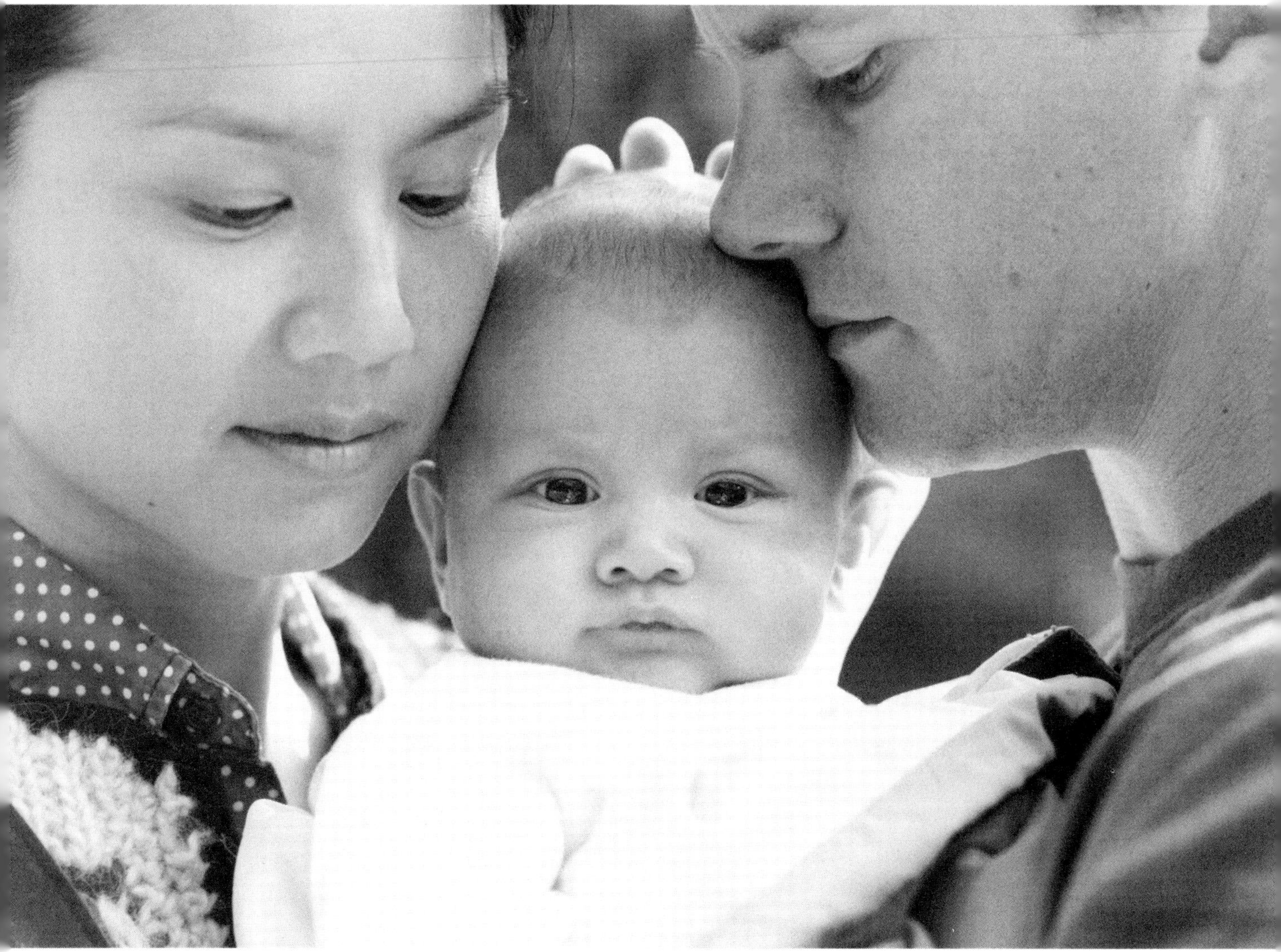

FAMILY

Few things can create more harmony and more disturbance in a family than a new baby. All of the various relationships in the family are shifted as the family makes space for a new person and everything that that new person will need and contribute. Children become parents, parents become grandparents, first children become siblings. Everybody's sense of themselves is affirmed and threatened at the same time.

  While as a mother you've felt your baby inside you for months, it's still a shock to actually have the baby in your arms needing to be fed and comforted. As a father you have even less of a sense of the baby before he's born or the work involved in taking care of him. A young child can act and feel very positive and excited about having a new baby in the family without having any idea what it really means to share his parents. New grandparents may feel as though they should be happy but also feel resentment at the confirmation that they're getting older and bewilderment about exactly how to contribute. Adding a new baby is unthinkably complex and profound, and it takes everyone some time to adjust.

  For your baby's sake, for your own sake, and for the sake of the rest of your family, try to take your time adjusting to the new arrival. Don't be too hard on your-

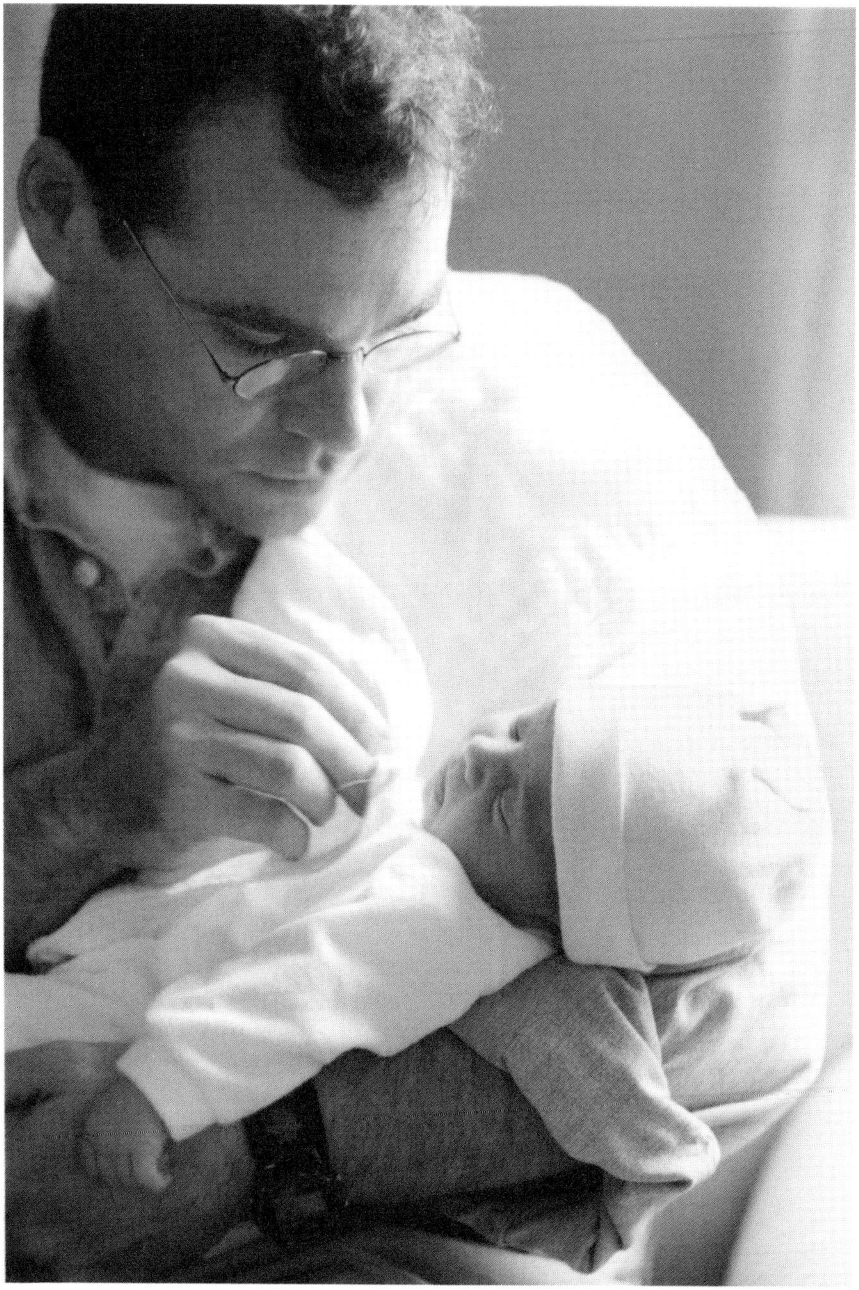

selves or each other if occasionally you wish you could go back in time. Don't make your first child spend too much time around the new baby. Don't expect your parents to jump into weekly competent baby-sitting right off the bat. During those first few weeks with a new baby, when everyone is tired and confused and sometimes very happy, try to get everyone to give everyone else a little extra understanding, and remember to have a little extra understanding yourselves.

FATHERS AND MOTHERS

As a new father you're also exhausted emotionally and physically from the birth. Suddenly you go from having all of your wife's attention to having practically none of it. Your normal wife became a round, moody baby-maker and then a deflated, sore, exhausted baby-lover. You're elated by having a baby and proud of your wife for giving birth, but you're also stunned by the reality of it all, unable to take over any of the physical transitions your wife is going through, and suddenly aware of your wife's and the baby's dependence on you and—somehow at the same time—independence from you. You miss your wife's attention sharply, you feel pressure to love the baby and pitch in at home, and you're not quite sure that anything will ever feel normal again.

One way to help yourself make a good transition from husband to husband-and-father, and to take your mind off being jealous of the baby is to help with the baby care right from the beginning. There is no inborn ability that women have for changing diapers or giving sponge baths. You can learn right along with the mother how to do these things so that you can feel the love and connection that comes through caring for the baby.

You should decide what you like to do best—take walks, sing, bottle-feed, bathe, diaper, or jiggle the carriage until the baby falls asleep—and then insist on doing it when you're home. This is easier to get started if the mother is not in sight, hearing, smelling, or advice-giving distance. Slowly, you and your baby will develop your own way of doing things and your own relationship, which will be invaluable to you both.

As a new mother you may feel as though you should be doing everything yourself, but you and your husband are a team, and the more you treat him as your partner, the better it will be for both of you. Help him to find out what he likes to do for the baby and for you, and let him do it. Give him plenty of time completely alone with the baby. Don't criticize his technique with the baby, his laundry ability, his choice of pizza for dinner. It's hard when you're tired and feeling overwhelmed, but remember to love him and appreciate him for his efforts. Let him forge his own way to a relationship with his baby.

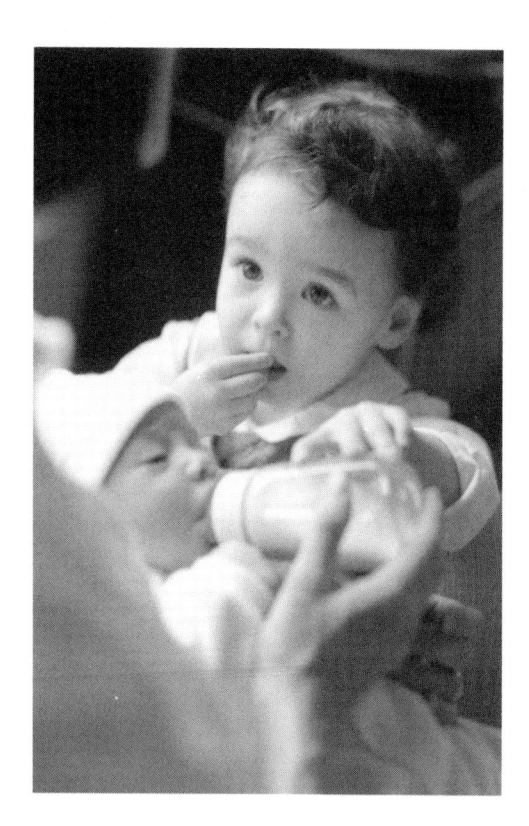

SIBLINGS

Oma strongly recommends introducing a new baby to a sibling very gradually. To begin with, don't talk about how great it's going to be to have a baby too much before the actual event. Until the baby comes it is really only an idea to the child, and if they get excited but then don't feel excited when the baby actually comes, they may feel bad about their feelings. Talk about it only occasionally and very matter-of-factly, and let it go at that.

There is no reason why a child needs to help bring you and the baby home from the hospital either. Remember that there are a few things going on simultaneously for the first child, one of which is

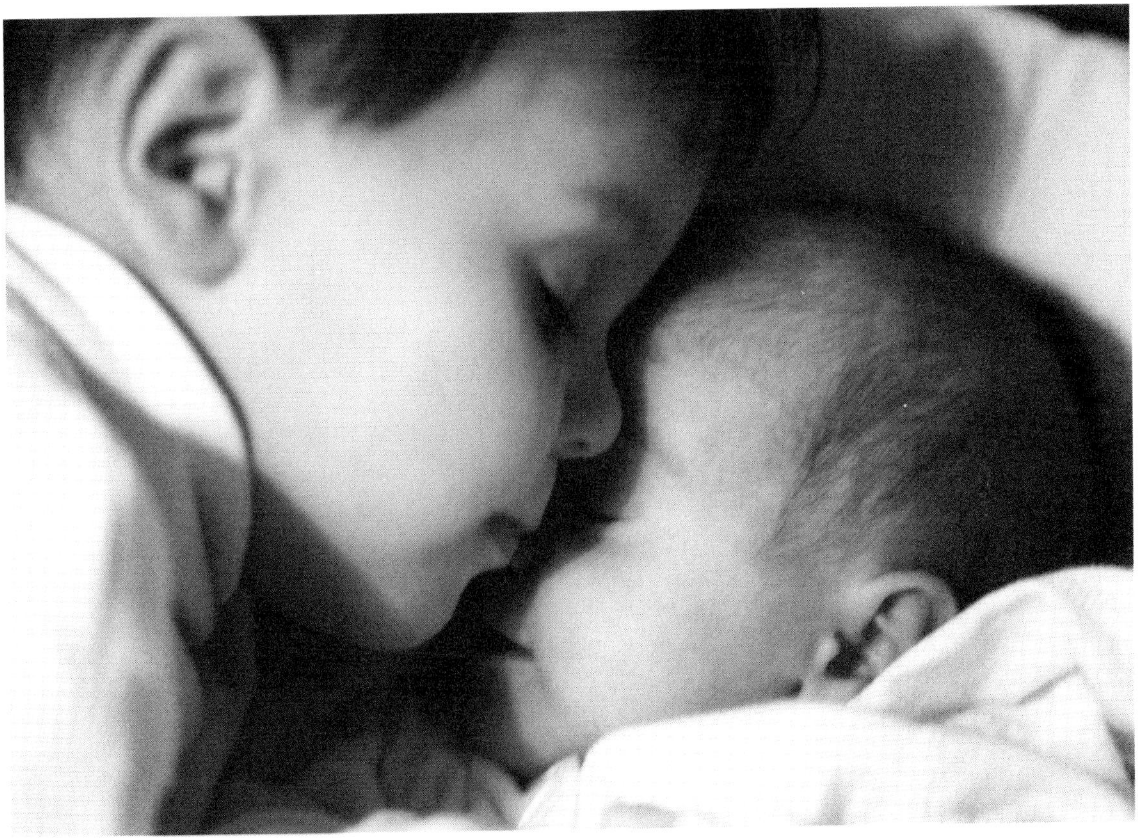

being worried about how she'll be treated. Chances are, when you come back from the hospital you will still have discomfort, and this will only add to the toddler's worries. If you can, let the toddler have a date with an aunt or uncle or friend and then come home to find an already-settled-in mother and father who are ready to pay attention to her.

Once both the baby and the child are under the same roof, let the toddler see the baby and the baby's care only gradually if possible. A toddler confronted with a nursing baby and mother ten times a day is bound to be a little upset, whereas it can be quite interesting for a toddler once or twice a day. Try to schedule one feeding before the toddler wakes up in the morning, one during her nap, and another after she goes to sleep at night. Perhaps the toddler can help with one more feeding by holding the bottle. This will leave only a few that she will see but won't be a part of.

At the same time, don't pretend that there is no baby, because there is and the first child will need to get accustomed to that. But let the child figure out for herself how she feels and discover the joy of having a baby without having it forced upon her. This is difficult when you want everyone to be happy right away, but in the long run your chances of having happily frolicking siblings is greater if you let them develop their own relationship.

Make sure your first child has plenty of attention from other adults and is able to play with children her own age as frequently as usual. This will confirm her sense of self, her budding independence, and her new identity as the big kid much more than being told, "You're the big kid now."

When your first child acts like a baby occasionally, be understanding, don't pay too much attention to it, and try not to expect her instantly to become a competent older sibling. Ignore or redirect jealous behavior in the toddler, and admire her loving behavior toward the baby when it happens. Don't label your toddler "jealous" or "impossible" in her presence, or she just may live up to your expectations.

Even once a good relationship seems to be growing between your toddler and your baby, never leave them together unattended. It is unfair to entrust a baby's well-being to a child, and if something went wrong you would not want the child to feel responsible, which she would. If you must leave a room where they both are, simply take one with you.

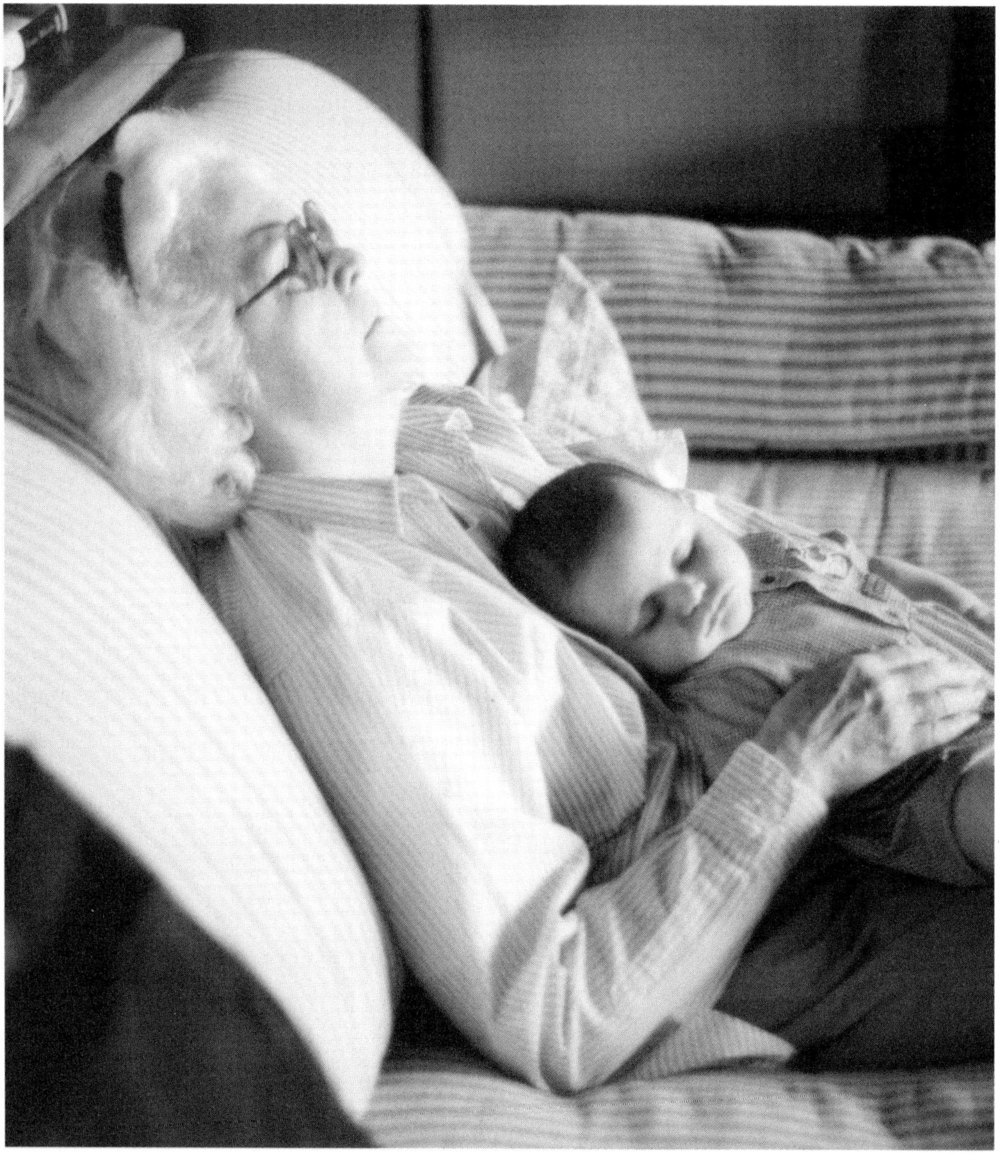

GRANDPARENTS

When you have a baby you suddenly have new status as a parent. At the same time your status as your parents' child is confirmed. Both you and your parents are reminded when a baby is born of the complete dependence of a baby on its parents. It can be a wonderful revelation to appreciate your parents and what they did for you, and it can also be paralyzing. Do they know best? When do your own ideas about parenting come into play? Should you listen to them or your pediatrician when their advice conflicts? Do you have to treat your in-laws as equals with your own parents now? It takes a few years or longer to sort out your own answers to these questions, so don't despair if you're confused at the beginning.

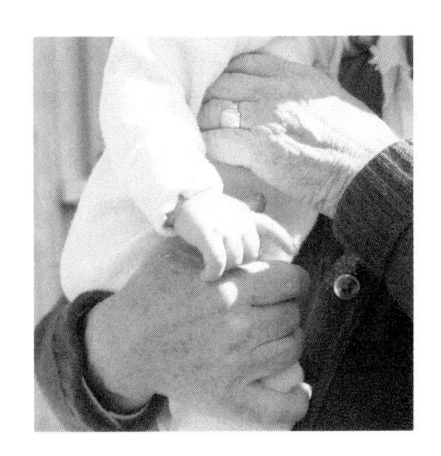

Oma recommends that you take advantage of any help that your parents can give you but also listen very carefully to your own intuition about your baby. At the beginning your intuition may be fragile, but it will be the foundation of your approach with your baby and you need to develop it. You will incorporate advice from many sources, but your intuition will tell you what will be right for you and your baby and what won't.

If you need a few days alone with each other and your baby, tell your parents. If you feel overwhelmed and want more help from the grandparents, tell them. Also be prepared to let them see their grandchild. After all, the baby is theirs too. Set a pattern from the start that you'll let them know what you want and need and that you want to know what they want and need. Work together, if possible, to find a balance that works for everyone without unspoken resentments. Remember that what seems obvious to you may not be obvious to them.

PETS

As with a sibling it is important to introduce a new baby to a family pet gradually. No matter how much you trust your pet, introducing a new baby into the family is a big disruption to his world, and it is your responsibility to supervise the transition. In the beginning a usually calm but jealous pet may unexpectedly attack a baby. An excitable puppy or kitten may want to "play" in a way that is harmful to a baby without knowing it. An older cat who loves the new baby may cuddle with him when he's asleep and suffocate him by accident. If your pet grew up in a household without small children, he may have extra trouble getting used to it.

Before bringing your baby home you need to bring your pet to a veterinarian for a complete checkup and any necessary shots. Then you need to form a plan for keeping the baby safe while letting your pet get used to him under strict supervision, which will last well into childhood. Oma offers the following approach:

- ☐ Have very short and few visiting sessions with the baby, and don't pressure your pet to love the baby.
- ☐ Make sure you keep paying attention to your pet, but not more than usual.
- ☐ Don't forget to feed your pet at the usual times and keep snacks handy for when you're feeding the baby (but make sure you wash your hands in between feeding the pet and feeding your baby).
- ☐ Use a monitor and *keep the nursery door closed* whenever your baby is asleep and you are elsewhere in the house or asleep.
- ☐ Take your dog with you when you go for walks and bring a ball or stick to play with (your baby will love this eventually).
- ☐ When your dog licks your baby, don't get angry (it's natural and affectionate); just wash your baby's face and hands with a cloth soon after.

Basically, use the same guidelines as for introducing a baby to an older sibling and be aware of your pet's feelings, but don't give him the idea that a wrong has been done him by overcompensating either. Give your baby and your pet a chance to form their own relationship.

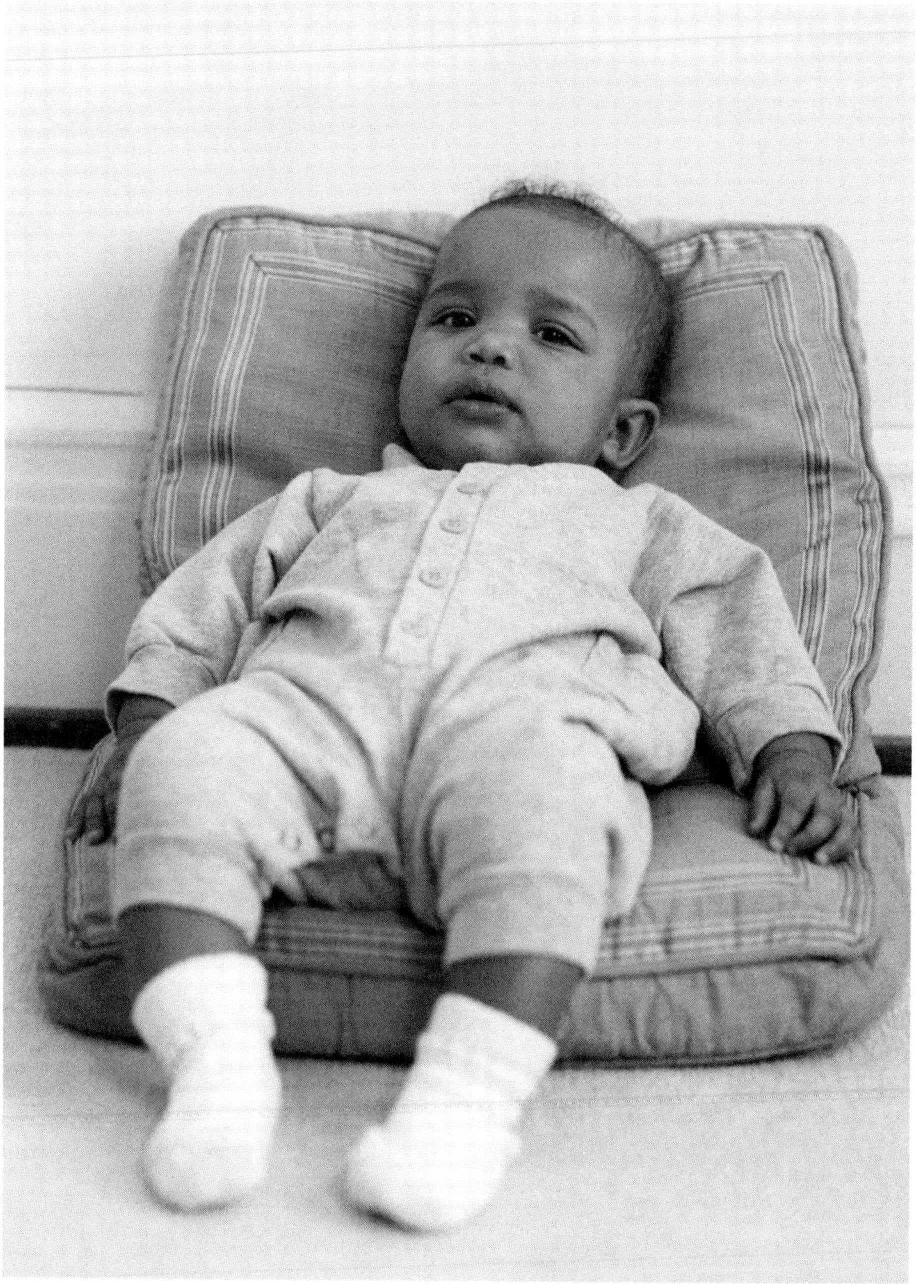

ILLNESS

Few things are as heartbreaking as an ill baby. You feel afraid, you might feel guilty, you want to do anything you can to make your baby well. Your role as a parent is to make sure you are receiving the best medical care possible for your baby and also to make sure your baby is as comfortable as possible and feels loved.

PICKING A PEDIATRICIAN AND DECIDING WHEN TO CALL

You need a pediatrician you can ask any question, no matter how seemingly trivial, and who will take the time to make sure you understand everything he or she is telling you. If you are afraid of your pediatrician or don't understand him, that will interfere with the open communication you need to have with him. Interview a few pediatricians you've heard good things about and then choose the one you're most comfortable with. You want to feel secure that your baby is receiving appropriate medical care so that you can concentrate on what only you can provide for your baby—comfort and love.

Judging how ill your baby is and when it's time to call the pediatrician is difficult at first. A good indicator of illness is the behavior of your baby. Is she interacting the way she usually does? Is she eating and making dirty diapers as usual? If not, you should probably call your pediatrician. The younger your baby is, the lower your threshold for calling the pediatrician should be.

FEVER

Fever is uncomfortable for your baby and is a sign of illness, but it is not in and of itself dangerous. If your baby is less than three months old and has a fever, call your pediatrician. But if your baby is more than three months old and is behaving normally, you should ask your pediatrician at what level of fever you should call him. If it's lower than that level, don't worry and concentrate on making your baby comfortable.

When you have a fever you feel cold as your temperature goes up and then you feel hot as your temperature goes down. This is because of the difference between your internal temperature and the room temperature. When your baby has a fever, keep in mind that she'll be feeling alternately hot and cold depending on what part of the temperature cycle she is in.

Oma suggests clean, smooth sheets and a cotton layer or two of blankets, but keep reevaluating how your baby feels. If she's sweaty make sure her skin can breathe to let off extra heat, but keep in mind that she'll feel cold, so make sure her feet are covered and you have a dry blanket to wrap her in.

Make sure you have a bottle of clean, cool water for your baby to sip to replace the fluids she's giving up with sweating.

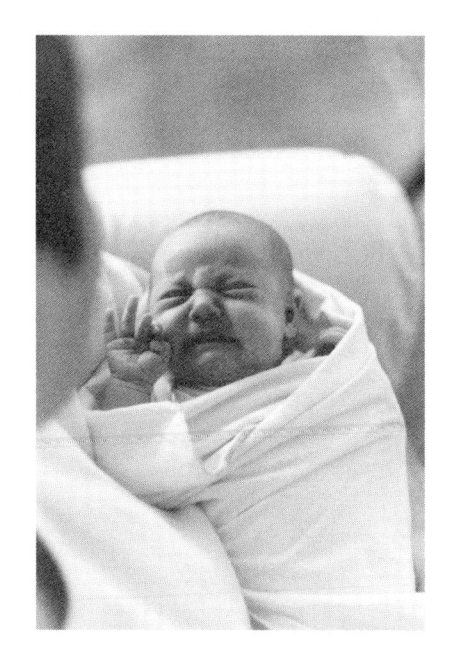

CONGESTION

Young babies do not know how to open their mouths on purpose to breathe when their noses are congested. They gasp, and then when they cry they get a breath. Nasal congestion is disruptive and uncomfortable for babies, but it isn't dangerous. There are a few short-term remedies for nasal congestion that are useful to help a baby eat and sleep. The first is suction. You can gently insert the tip of a suction ball into your baby's nose and try to remove as much mucus as you can. This is pretty difficult though. An easier method is to tilt your baby's head back *slightly* and drop one drop of clean water into each nostril. Bring her back upright and let her sneeze. Oftentimes this will clear the nose just enough for a baby to suck some milk and get some rest.

Another way to ease the pressure of a stuffed nose is to run a hot shower, close the bathroom door, and sit with your baby in the steam.

A good way to ease the pressure of congestion for your baby when she's lying in her crib is to raise the head end of the crib mattress a bit by putting a book or two on top of the box spring and under the head of the mattress. This helps fluids drain out of her nose and sinuses. Don't try to put books under the feet of the crib, because the crib might fall off them.

Oma recommends that all through the winter you keep one or two towels out of the dryer when you do laundry and hang them over a drying rack in your baby's room near a radiator. This will provide a continuous source of moist air for your baby without the mold that can sometimes grow in humidifiers. If you do use a humidifier, use a cool-mist type and clean the filter with white vinegar to kill mold.

SURROUNDINGS

When your baby is sick, chances are she's feeling as irritable as the rest of us feel when we're sick. Maybe sounds are louder in her ears, maybe she's uncomfortable being handled. Maybe she wants to be held more. Try to get to know your baby's needs when she's sick, keeping in mind that they might be quite different from her well needs. Make sure her clothes are comfortable and breathable and dry, make sure her feet are warm, make sure her head is elevated at least a bit when she's awake. When changing your ill baby's diaper make sure the room is warm enough so that she won't get chilled.

Sometimes a little gentle distraction—such as a turn around the apartment in a stroller or some music—can help a baby feel better, but watch out for making your baby overtired when she's ill. Oftentimes just lying next to your baby on a bed and reading or watching a quiet video is soothing for an ill baby. Massage her legs and arms a little to stimulate circulation before she has another nap.

Occasionally an ill baby can cause stress between parents. When you're both worried and your baby is making more demands on you both than you're accustomed to, you have to try to remember that it will pass and that you're both concerned for the baby and are trying to help in your own way.

Oma makes a point of making "sick" time a special time. If you see it as a chance to get cozy together and indulge in extra stories and snuggling, as a break from your usual schedule, you and your spouse and your baby will be less worried.

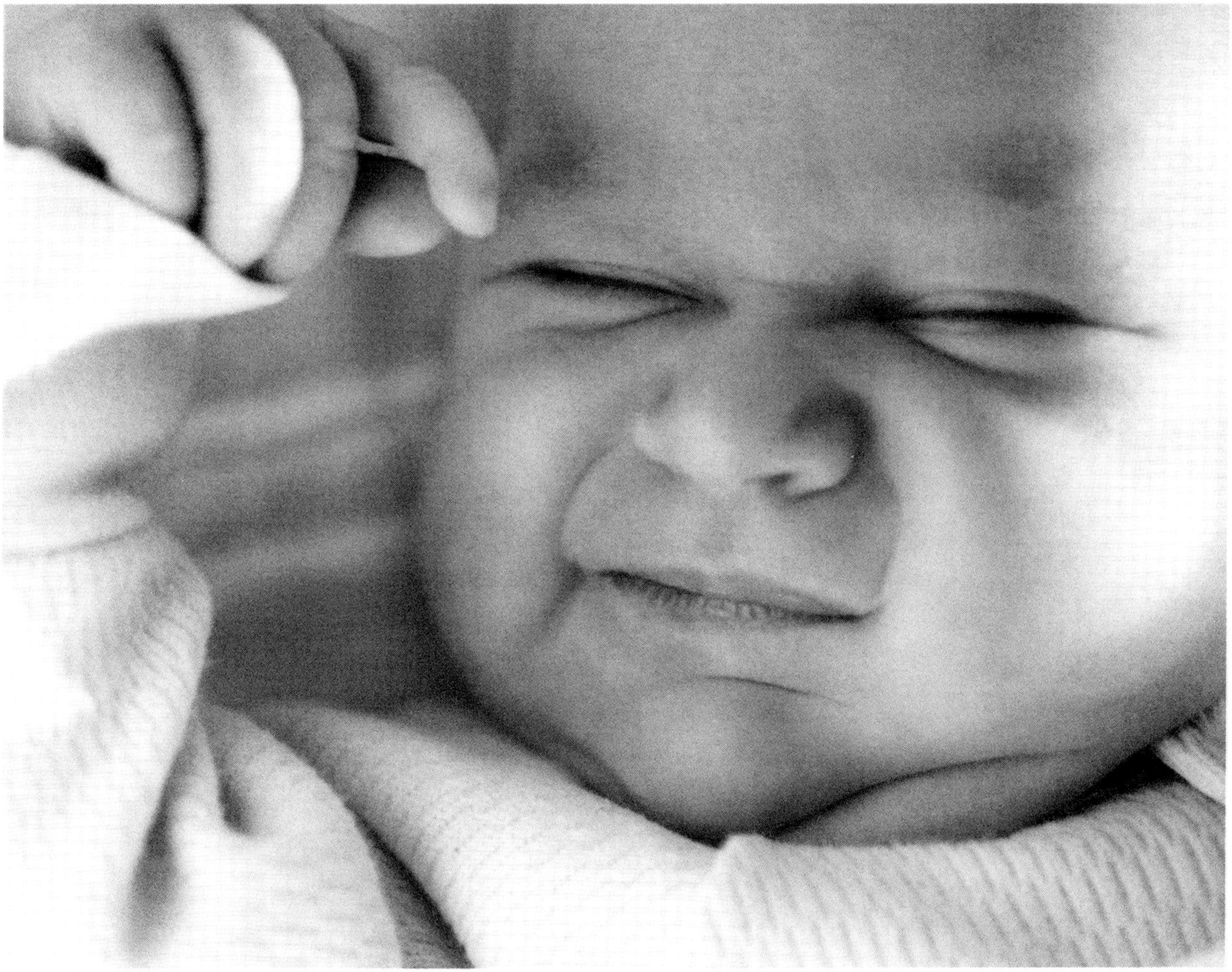

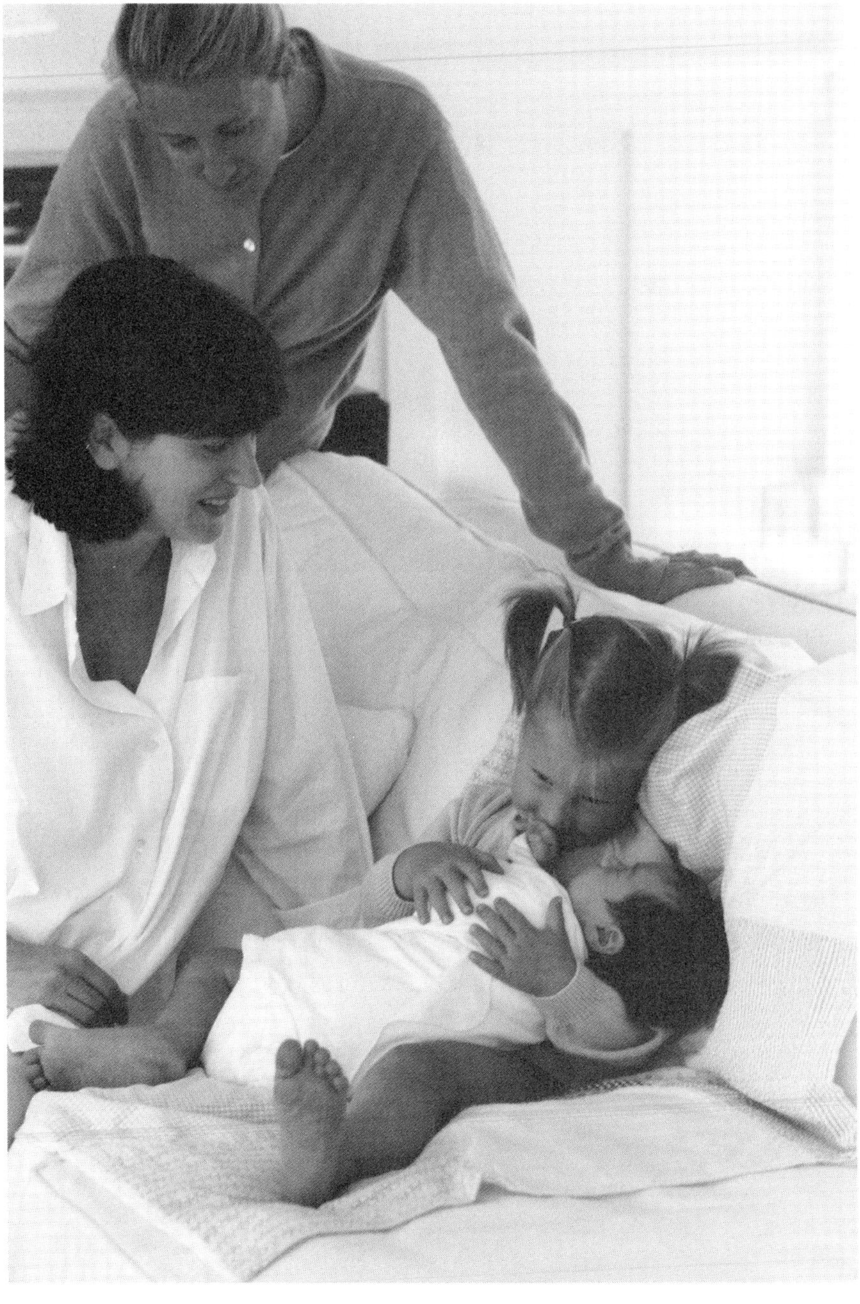

VISITORS

Having a baby is such an intense and personal event that sometimes you forget that it's an event for other people too. For your best friend it might be a rite of passage or your entrance into the Parents' Club. For your neighbor it's an opportunity to show generosity and good will. For your boss it's a corporate event and an anxiety-provoking disturbance of scheduling. People will react in a variety of ways to your having a baby, and much of what they'll do may be incomprehensible or annoying to you. It's good to remember that your baby affects a lot of people and that you'll need to be understanding.

And they'll visit. They'll want to hold your baby, kiss her, and they'll try their hardest to make her smile. If you're as prepared and organized about visitors as any other part of taking care of your baby, you may even enjoy them.

PICK A TIME FOR VISITORS TO COME

If you're not organized you'll find out very quickly that people will call and visit at all the wrong times. If you think about it you'll realize that actually there are very few good times for people to visit. You need to decide what these times are.

You want to take into account whether or not the baby will be awake. You may want visiting time to be when your baby is awake so that people can see her eyes open, but you should realize that if she's awake she may need to eat or have her diaper changed, neither of which are visitors' favorite things to watch. Oma believes in having people visit when the baby is asleep and when you've already had a nap. That way your visitors can peek in at the baby ("Shhhh, let's not wake her up"), they'll get your full attention, and everyone will be happy with a reassurance that in a few weeks the baby will be awake more often.

One of the benefits of having a scheduled visiting time is that more than one visitor can come at once. Don't feel bad about not providing an exclusive "viewing" for each visitor. Handling visitors is a good way to practice putting your baby's needs first. And one of your baby's needs is having a mother who gets rest. There are only so many times during the first few weeks of your baby's life that you'll be looking presentable and feeling up to making conversation. The more visits you can take care of at once, the better. Many people will be satisfied by a telephone call and the promise of a visit when the baby is a few weeks old.

HAVE A PLAN

Once you've decided on good times for you to have visitors, stick to it.

If you or your husband have trouble saying no to people, let the outspoken one answer the calls and have a script ready, which could read something like this:

"It's so nice of you to want to visit. The best time(s) would be _____."

"Well, we really can handle visitors only at _____. We would really like to see you then."

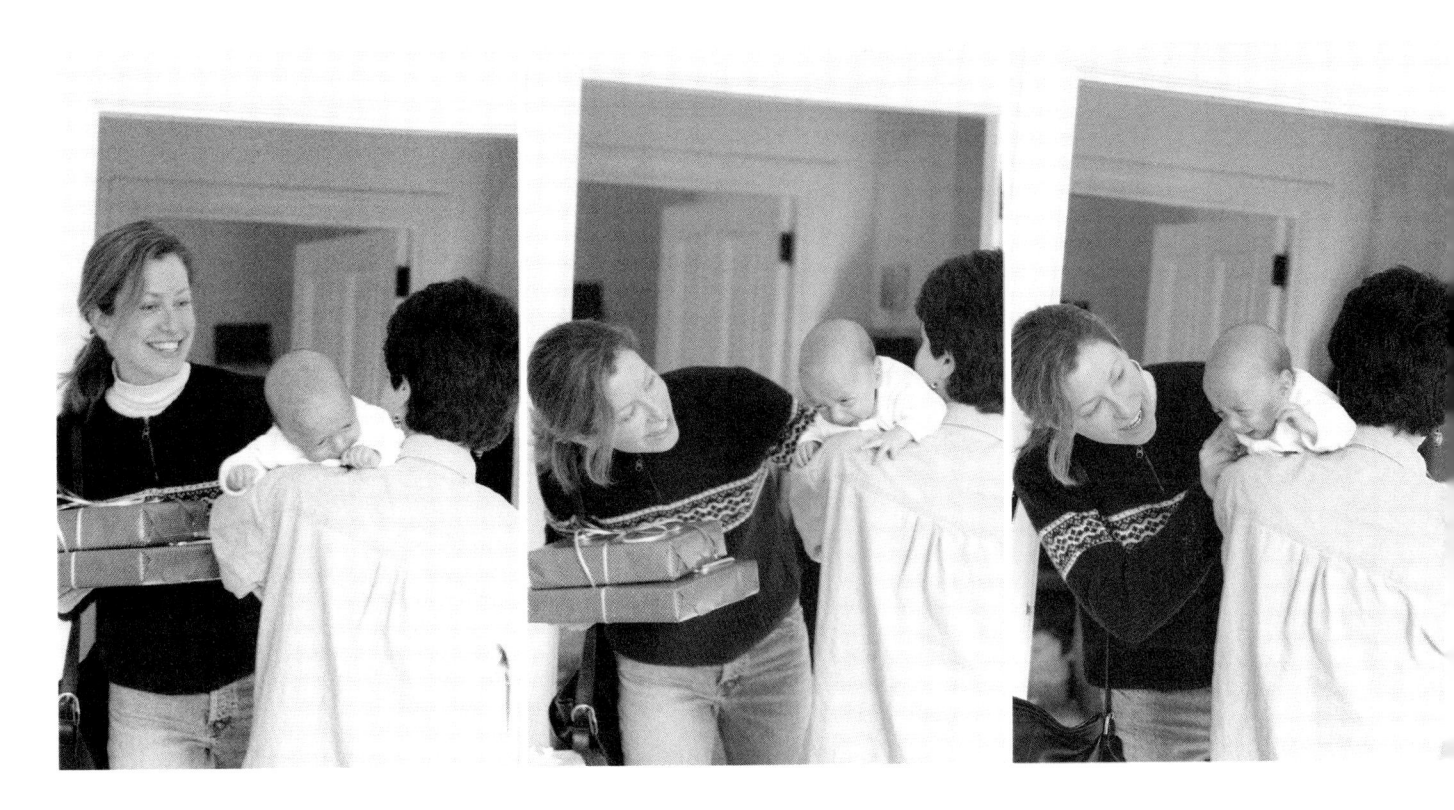

"Well, maybe next week then. The baby will be more awake then also. That would be nice."

People do want to see your baby, of course, but they also just want to be sure that you know that they care and that they're making an effort.

It's good to have two of you there for the visits also. Remember that people who don't have babies won't understand exactly how tired you are and they might expect coffee or other things, which can become difficult. It helps if one of you can play host so that the other can just sit and receive, holding the baby or not, and not jump up every two minutes.

RULES FOR VISITORS

Usually when people come into your house you can overlook certain things in the interest of hospitality, but if your visitors come when your baby is awake, there are three things you must insist on:

- ☐ Your guests must wash their hands before touching the baby.

- ☐ They must put a cloth over their shoulder if they are going to hold the baby, so that the baby doesn't suck on or breathe in whatever they are wearing.

- ☐ They must not come if they are ill, because your baby is very susceptible to getting sick and illnesses are usually more severe for a baby than for an adult.

Your primary responsibility as a parent is to keep your child safe, and the sooner you make that clear to yourself and get over being shy about it with others the fewer regrets you'll have later.

It might feel odd asking people to take these precautions, but if you treat it matter-of-factly and assume that they want to, you'll be surprised by how easy it is. If you don't know how to ask, you might try the following:

"There's a clean towel in the bathroom for your hands. Oh, I can't wait for you to hold her."

"Of course you need to wash your hands. It was so nice of you to come over. I want her to know you from the beginning."

"Here's a cloth for your shoulder, just in case she spits up." (This always works, and it's true anyway.)

"I'm sorry you have a cold—can you come the minute you get better? Let me show you pictures of her. That's so nice of you to call even though you're sick."

Just tell people what they have to do and then move on to another topic. Leave this book open to this page in a visible place.

When you have visitors who aren't used to handling babies, especially newborns with wobbly heads, it's a good idea to wrap your baby as a *pakje* with the blanket supporting her head (see "Crying"). Almost anyone can hold a *pakje* in their arms, and your baby will feel more secure being passed around this way.

The final rule for visitors is the following:

- They must leave.

Be honest about how worn out you are and that you can't handle a long visit. Your rest at this stage is very important both for you and for your baby. Oma's method is to say, "Well, I need to go feed the baby now" as a closer and then show your guests out. If they insist on waiting, then take the baby into another room to feed her a bottle or breast milk lying down (see "Food") and let your husband take over, explaining, "She eats better when it's very quiet," or leave your guest alone and she'll get the hint. Don't let the fact that you're bottle feeding interfere with using feeding time as an excuse to rest.

For the next few months your time will be dominated by taking care of your baby and getting to know her and trying to save some attention for each other, so don't try to pretend to your friends that you still have just as much time for them as you used to. Reassure them (and yourself) that your baby won't always need as much time as she does right now, but for now she does and you hope they will come to understand. By the same token, do schedule time with your friends and without your baby on occasion. It will help your attitude toward all of your new obligations immensely, and it will reassure them that you are still people in your own right.

KEEPING UP WITH THANK-YOU NOTES AND PICTURES

This may sound a little *too* organized, but before your baby is born you should buy at least a small box of thank-you cards. After the baby comes, the last errand you're going to want to do is to go to a stationery store, and silly as it may seem, that could be the biggest hurdle to your getting out thank-you notes. As visitors come by, keep a list of visitors and gifts so that you don't have to rely on your memory for thank-you notes.

And everyone is going to want a picture of your baby. Don't try to get a perfect picture of your baby holding the gift from each person. If that's your goal you'll never even pick up your camera. Likewise, if you pick a picture you like and then expect to get fifty copies of it made to send out, you probably won't get around to it until your baby is six months old. The easiest thing to do is to load your camera, lay your baby down on a nice blanket on the floor, pick a good angle (usually straight on or from a little above her eye level), and take a roll of pictures all at once. When you get them developed at the grocery store (where you have to go anyway), get double prints made. Then you'll have seventy-two prints to tuck into thank-you notes, and you'll nip in the bud all those telephone conversations that begin with, "When do I get to see a picture?"

If you send out two cards a day with very short messages (and that's easier to do with a picture enclosed), then you'll find it's not too hard to keep up to date.

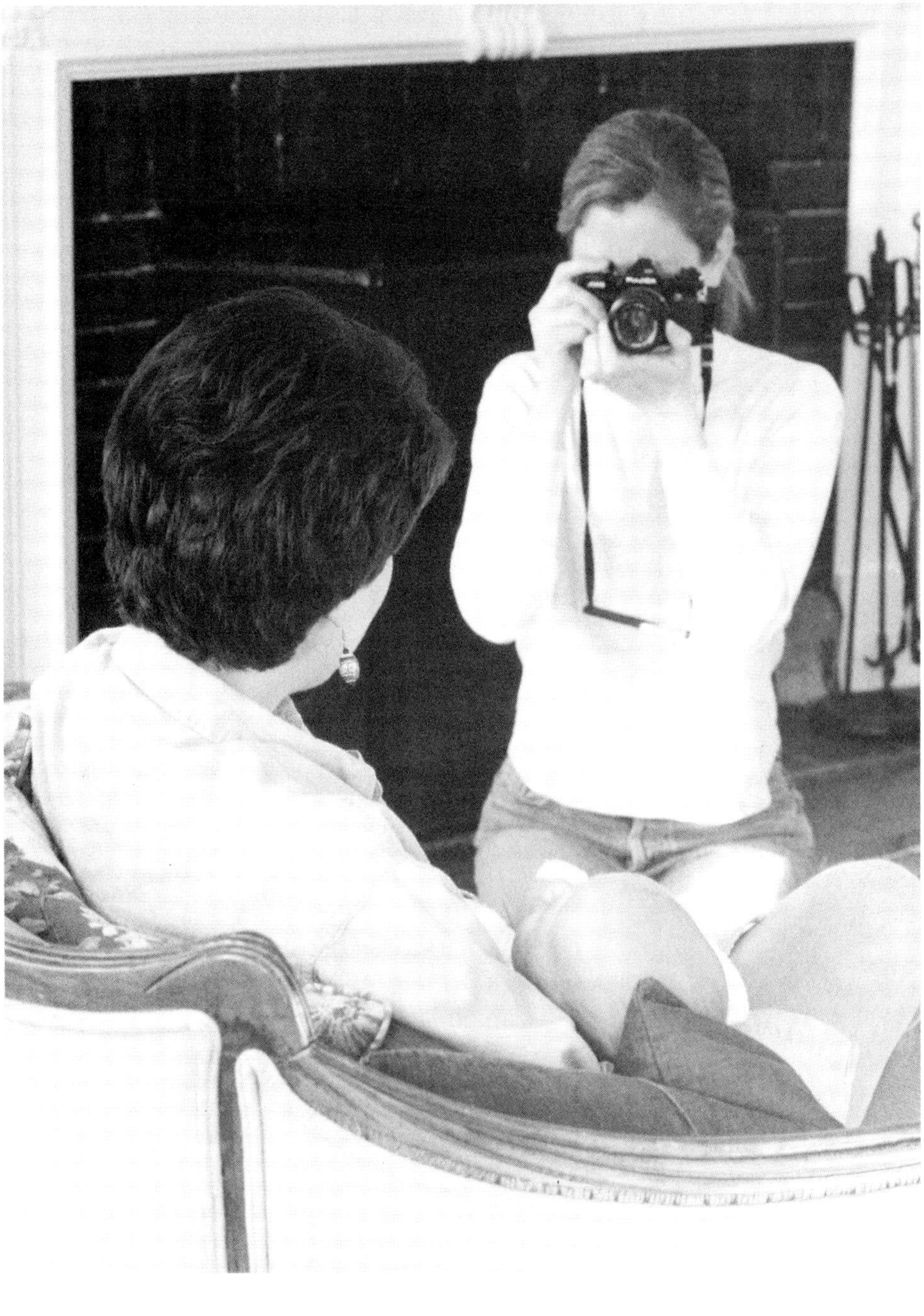

TIME TO GO TO SLEEP

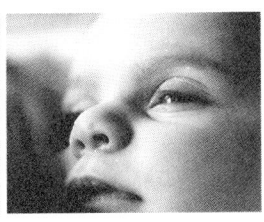

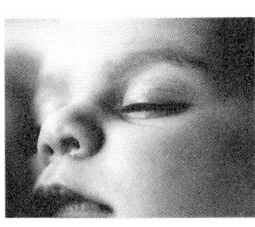

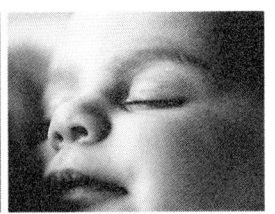

―――

When tears are cried
and songs are sung;
when milk is down;
when cheeks are kissed,
and toes are tickled,
and all the toys are put away;
when noses are wiped
and dishes clean,
and all the laundry folded,
or not,
it's time to go to sleep.

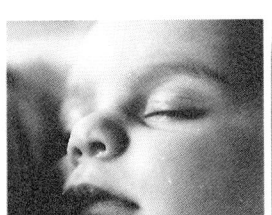

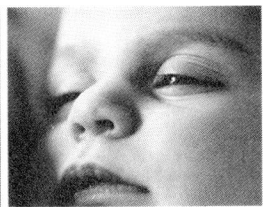

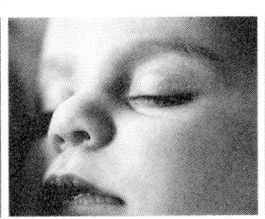

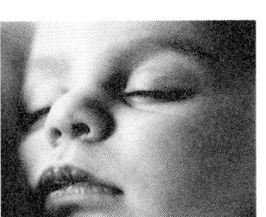

Maud Bryt is a professional photographer, mother of two, and wife of a pediatrician. She lives in New York. This is her first book.